Dedicated to Yaviz Basalamah.

You remain a rare, undeniable, beautiful, brilliant,

creative light in the world.

I miss you every day.

And to my Fabulous Friends, Fans, Superstars,

and Students.

For seeing me as some part of your journey

Towards Greater Love and Greater Wisdom,

Thank You.

Disclaimer: This book in no way provides medical advice. The author

and publisher advise and encourage seeking professional, medical

advice, insight, and assistance for any and all ailments or questions,

physical, psychological, or otherwise.

Table of Contents

Astrology As Spiritual Revolution

Astrology is, at its root, intimately tied to the development and evolution of human spiritual understanding. It is a living tool, adapting to the culture it finds itself in, in order to best serve the people who use it. Our orientation to the sky represents how we understand ourselves as human beings, our power and our potential. Astrology has been made stronger and been expanded upon by every culture and religion, ancient, historical, or contemporary. Whether past, present, or future, when we practice astrology, we are part of them all.

This is the definition of the New Age—an understanding that essentially, we are all from the same place. All the practices and wisdom of the world are available to any of us. Who we are can transcend the limiting, superficial definitions of ethnicity, religion, race, creed, or even of gender or orientation, and move towards a definition that puts our individual spiritual journey and our spiritual energy first and foremost. We are all on this path. We are united in this and so much more.

Astrology, for me, provides a small glimpse into the great mystery, revealing this great truth — "The Universe is Wise and Loving." It is ultimately only a glimpse, revealing only what it is that is ours to know at this time and what we are ready to see. Astrology is a tool that allows for clearer vision. It is a perfect mirror, reflecting what is happening here in our world and in our lives, interpreted by the imperfect human translation provided by the astrologer. It is esoteric knowledge, the kind we have to work to obtain. We each have a right to decide on our own relationship with the Divine, and therefore the sky, however we understand it. We have all been provided the tools to learn from our environment and appreciate our interconnectedness to everyone and everything.

Astrology is not a gift available only to the special select few. It is a skill, and like any skill, it takes time and patience to learn the first steps. However, the longer you practice, the better at it you get. Astrology can be learned by virtually anyone, and if you feel a calling to it, then it is your right to cultivate your own relationship to the sky. I affirm this for many reasons, but especially because of the philosophical assertion it makes. I do believe, very passionately, that each of us has a right to decide what the Divine, the Beloved, or the Universe — or whatever we call or however we understand that energy of love that unites us all—means to us; we each have a right to decide our relationship to it in our own individual lives.

The Universe is Synchronistic

It happened quite by accident, or more likely synchronicity. My professor at the time, Patrick Curry, told me to think of the library as a place of divination. If I moved through the place with trust and intuition, I would be led to the resources and information I needed. He suggested I establish an intention, and then browse the racks with an open heart.

I found myself in the section having to do with mystical religions, and then the more precise corner of Sufi writers. I knew that I came from a long line of Sufis, though I didn't personally practice myself, or have working knowledge of the tradition. Still, there were many stories, like myths in my mind, about who did what. The great uncle who was an artist and poet. The distant cousins who were musicians who meditated with Qawwali. The great-great grandparent occultist who lost his competition with spirits. The healers, the mystics, and the alchemists that dotted the family tree going back a millennium and a half.

Within the books, I found a series of small essays and impressive translations of a mystic who lived long ago, Ibn ʿArabi. One of his key concepts was what he called "The Magnificent Breath." Arabi believed that we are the breath of the Divine. He said that every emotion, fear, longing, or elation that we feel is another way that the creator knows itself more fully. And if we had not been there to experience that exact feeling, then that breath would be complete. What Arabi called God, was actually an energy that lived, breathed, and grew through our human experience. What we call God is the entirety, and the best that humanity can be. What Arabi called God, I came to call Love and Wisdom.

Arabi was also an astrologer. He believed that the chart was perfect. The aspects that you curse, that you wish were not there, are exactly what they need to be, so that you can do everything you've been created to do in the highest, most loving, and most fulfilled version of your life.

If you are familiar with my work, you've likely heard me say the phrase "The Universe is Wise and Loving" before. This phrase was my personal guiding mantra. At some point, it became evident in my work. Affirming this sacred truth is what I believe I am meant to do in this lifetime—for now.

It may seem Pollyannaish on the surface. How could it be possible to think of all things as part of a wise and loving Universe when there were real injustices in the world? Sigmund Freud believed that until we accept what he called "the cruelty of fate," we are never truly adults able to interact with life on its own terms.

There is a powerful distinction between what we want to believe, and how it is that we are meant to grow towards all that we could become.

For me, affirming a Universe that is wise and loving is ultimately what we are here to learn more about. It is what we are here to embody. What I call "Love and Wisdom" can also be called divine energy, creation energy, divinity, God, or the gods. It is this very energy that we are here to grow more into, to move towards, and to become in each of our moments as we live our lives. Every single person on this planet is moving towards this embodiment, though some hide it under layers of anger and pain. Others are more forthright in this journey.

The Nodes can be considered a higher, more karmic intent of the planet they are connected to. I believe the Nodes of the Moon are key to understanding what this path towards greater love and greater wisdom may be for you. More importantly, as the Moon in the chart represents what you need to be at peace with yourself, my hope is that in this moment, and with this perspective on the Nodes of the Moon, you are led to see how Love, Wisdom, and Peace are unfolding in your life now.

Astrology as an Act of Resistance

Astrology is, for me, a deeply spiritual practice. I see the planets and stars reveal their symbols to me more fully when I am willing to learn about them and cultivate that relationship. I disclose that in the few sentences I share with my audience to the best of my ability in this moment. That is what I have to give today, what I have to share, which will change and evolve as all things do.

People like me who present horoscopes each have our own way of communicating what we see, and that will resonate with our own audience. Different people like different interpretations. Some love poetic and psychological interpretations, while other people want to read astrology with a more literal interpretive communication style. With astrology being such a direct, applied, and intimate spiritual practice with such sacred roots, there are also unique ways of understanding the symbols and stressing the importance of one aspect over another. It will depend on the astrologer, and what they bring to their practice, and this, in turn, determines their audience.

There are a variety of techniques that go into writing horoscopes. The main one, of course, is solar charts. That is, putting the Sun for the sign I am writing in the first house and considering the sky from that perspective. There is the consideration of ruling planets and the aspects they are making. Just like many writing styles out there and just like the many astrologers out there, there are many techniques that allow us to cast a judgment and deliver an omen that will, in some way, be meaningful for the reader. I get about forty words per sign to do this for the day, the week, the month, or the year. It is an extraordinary challenge, but those of us who write Sun signs know from the feedback we receive that it can have a way of speaking something true to the life experience of the reader.

The most important thing for me is not so much what astrologers do as what we represent. And what we as Sun-sign columnists represent.

Astrology is one of the only ancient practices that is still a widespread part of popular, mass culture today. It has survived because, on some level, it affirms our connection with our immediate and larger environment. We are no longer just alienated, random creatures existing in the "iron cage of post modernism" (to borrow Max Weber's term), but part of a larger rhythm and cycle that has significance and purpose to it.

As articulated by Patrick Curry, with astrology, even when only considered entertainment, the understanding of ecology, as in the belief that the world is alive and therefore worthy of our respect, is further reinforced. That little horoscope, those two sentences read in the back of a magazine, have that deep a philosophical root that is reaffirmed in a very quiet, unassuming way.

Sun-sign astrology is one of the only ways this message is affirmed for many people, if not the overwhelming majority of people who encounter astrology. Of course, those forty words of an astrologically inspired omen can never take the place of a full consultation, but the columnist makes the likelihood for a consultation rise exponentially. Astrology isn't some foreign, strange, scary practice for our new clients, but something they have encountered in their local newspaper and magazine. Sun-sign columns can therefore open one doorway to a process for our entire astrological community to much more likely grow more fans, a small number of whom may eventually become astrologers themselves. Sun-sign columnists are a huge part of what has kept astrology in the mainstream. When we, as writers, are guided by love, and honor the techniques to our practice, we also maintain our personal integrity. If there is any obligation to astrology as a whole, it is to do what we can to educate people on the beauty of our practice and its value to our larger culture. The entryway to this educational process can begin with the Sun-sign columnist who can speak to the heart of his or her readers.

For me, that is important. I love being a part of all of that. I love reminding people that they are part of a larger mystery, and that all lives are meaningful. The sky is, ultimately, impartial. It just is— shining above us, acting as a mirror to help us better understand ourselves and our choices. Everyone is loved exactly where they are, right now, in this moment, going through whatever challenge or blessing that is visiting for the time. Astrology is a gentle reminder that there is a bigger unknown that everyone and everything is a part of, and that choosing to live in alignment with the patterns and progressions of life is one very powerful way of making one's life truly their own.

For this and so much more, I love being a part of astrology. I am passionate about what and all I do in service to astrology, and also dedicated to why I do it.

Why We Do All We Do

No matter what happens to us, from injustices, to hurts, disappointments and sadness, as human beings, we have the ability to find meaning and wisdom in all things. We can choose an interpretation that serves us, that moves us towards greater love and wisdom. All things can move us towards living fuller lives of greater compassion and contribution, as I believe they are meant to.

In my own life, I have seen how disappointing experiences with others can dampen the spirit. No matter how small and insignificant, these encounters painfully loom large in the mind. But even though these people behaved in ways that felt at the time as insensitive or mean, with hindsight these very people and experiences revealed themselves to eventually to be a great blessing. They set the stage for me to move further in the direction I was meant to go in, towards greater joy, fulfillment, compassion and service.

I'm grateful to all the Friends and Fans, both those who have been with me since the start and those who have just found their way to these pages. Your growth, interactions, and suggestions contribute to the evolution of my work.

I am constantly looking to find new ways to do what it is I believe I am meant to do, which is to affirm in the world, "The Universe Is Wise and Loving"

The mission of all my work, and of everything you find on my website, is to affirm in whatever way I am inspired or led to that "The Universe Is Wise and Loving." That's it. That is, to the best of my knowledge, my purpose and mission in this lifetime. It is first and foremost in each day, and in this is my work, which is also my love, and the expression my soul has found to express that love.

My intention is to constantly find new ways to live this mission, to trust the direction that shows me how to live it, even when I can't see all the details immediately, and to believe that my life and work, in some way, contributes to the chorus of voices rising from the depths of the oldest souls that have ever walked this Earth as they remind us who we really are.

And that is part of what this book is about for me. It's about seeing how, even in the hardest or most confusing times in our lives, whether in the midst of them or after they have passed, there is something there that promises its usefulness to us. There is something in everything that we can use to consciously move ourselves towards greater love and greater wisdom, always. It's not always the easy choice—in fact, the greater the wisdom, the more love we have to bring to choose it. And yet, the promise is there to move powerfully in the direction of greater embodiment of these very greater values.

Exploring the Nodes has been a powerful way of contemplating the ways in which we are constantly evolving, in sometimes unknown or surprising ways. They are a powerful reminder of the roots of astrology as a practice developed by some of the great goat shamans, marsupial philosophers, and meandering mystics to ever walk the Earth, for there is no higher calling than the desire to contemplate wisdom and consciously strengthen the energy of love and nurturing within. An awareness of our Nodes, which in lived experience plays out on levels of the unconscious and of spirt, is a powerful tool to cultivate alignment with these higher principles and outcomes of a life that is useful, more meaningful, more impactful, and well lived.

The Universe is wise and loving. This is the ultimate motivation of the Universe. It is our ultimate aim, our collective move towards this realization and reality. When I look at the sky, I see in symbolic form how this is all playing out. How each experience is inviting us to choose to be part of the ebb or the flow, all in the inevitable, ultimate direction of this greater embodiment.

My hope is that this book serves as a reminder of your unique place in this constant shared evolution that we participate in together. That you remember that it is love that is at your very core. Love is your very nature, and it is wisdom that awakens it. My hope is that learning about the Nodes helps you to more adamantly and unabashedly commit to the truly rewarding path of amplifying love and wisdom, as it lives, grows, and breaths in you now and always.

Understanding The Nodes As Love And Wisdom

All planets have Nodes. They represent key moments as part of a planet's journey along the ecliptic that the planet will travel in the sky. The Nodes are not physical bodies in the sky but are considered chart points in astrology. These are points of intersection that hold special sensitivity, with symbolic and archetypal significance.

Symbolically, the Nodes speak to the higher, spiritual intention of that planet. Some systems of astrology, like Evolutionary Astrology, utilize the Nodes of the different planets with special emphasis. In my view, the higher spiritual intent of all the planets and all the cosmos is to move us towards greater love and greater wisdom. Just as Ibn 'Arabi states that we are the incarnation of the Magnificent Breath, I do believe it is this full embodiment of divine energy that is the underlying motivation to all we are and all we do. Every lesson we learn, every karmic contract we fulfill, allows us to grow our spirt, as part of this very breath, more magnificent than it was before. This is the work that we have incarnated to do, and the planets are a symbolic representation of how we might go about doing this on conscious levels of awareness.

The Nodes become especially revealing because they speak to the unconscious, yet most obvious ways we might go about this ultimate thrust of the spiritual intent. We are here to more fully embody love and wisdom, to the best of our human ability, over the course of this lifetime. The Nodes can reveal to us how and where some of the most obvious pathways can be revealed, towards fulfilling this higher intention of this lifetime.

Because the Nodes speak to karmic promises, karmic and soul contracts, and the spiritual intention of that planet, they can be used as a powerful tool in prediction. The Nodes activated by transit are one of the strongest indicators of events transpiring in our lived experience. Changes can seem especially fated. People come and go, opportunities arrive, and closures take place as the Nodes are activated.

The Moon represents what we need to be at peace with ourselves. It is our comfort zone, or what we understand as the feeling of "home." The Moon is how and where, based on sign and house placement, that we go about seeking and reaching emotional equilibrium. There is a restorative quality to honoring our Moon. Whatever success might happen in the outer world, it means little if we are not at peace with ourselves. In this way, I find the Moon to be intimately tied to life purpose, because when we are seeking to align with our purpose, very often, what we are truly wanting is to feel at peace with ourselves. The Moon points the way to finding the inner reconciliation that defines being truly at peace within our body, within our skin, and feeling at home as we move through the world.

The Nodes of the Moon are the most widely used planetary Nodes in astrology. Taking the symbolic importance of the Moon into consideration, I find it especially intriguing that the Nodes of the Moon are the nodal staple where it comes to engaging them in astrological practice. Astrology is a living practice. It has evolved many times, becoming whatever the historical context or a given culture needs it to be. Interpretations evolve and expand, becoming more personal and relevant to the people within a given society. Even with all the shifts, changes, and revolutions within this practice, the importance of the Nodes of the Moon has remained constant.

The planets speak to what we want, why we want it, and how we go about getting it. The Moon is the conscious part of us that has learned, through demonstration and nurturance, what home looks and feels like. But the Nodes are more profound. It is as if the ancients understood that honoring the higher intention of the part of us that seeks peace is a powerful pathway towards honoring the spiritual intuition of this lifetime.

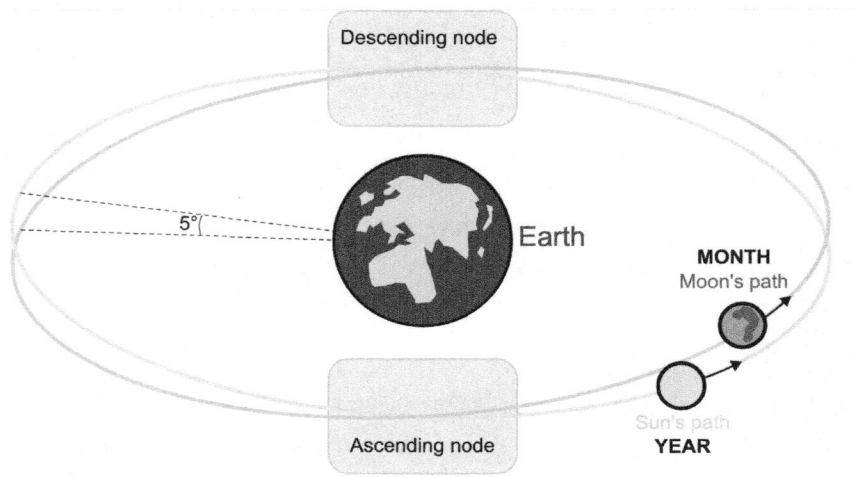

Scientifically, Noah Frere explains, "The Nodes of the Moon are points where the path of the Moon crosses the path of the Sun (the ecliptic). The North Node is where the Moon is traveling northwards (towards the North Pole) across the ecliptic, and the South Node is where the Moon travels towards the South Pole, always exactly opposite the North Node. After crossing the North Node, the Moon continues northward for about a week until it reaches its maximum northward point above the ecliptic, at which point it turns around and heads southward toward the ecliptic again."

The Head and Tail of The Dragon

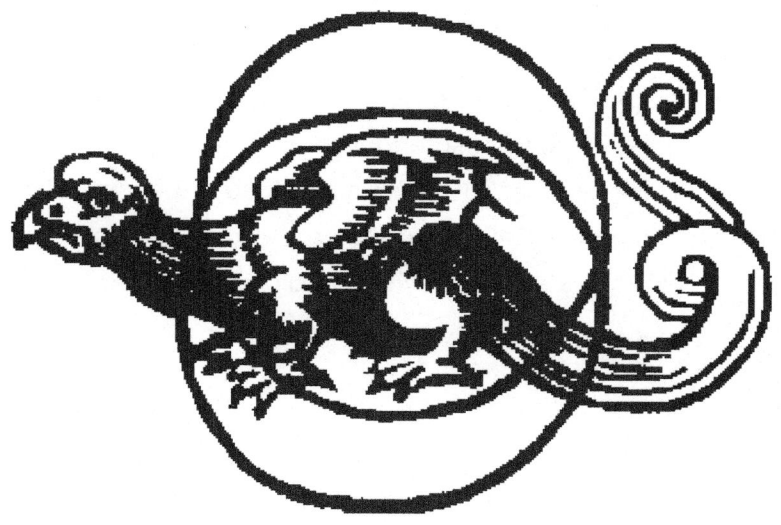

In *The 3 Books of Occult Philosophy*, Agrippa advises us on how to understand and interpret the Nodes of the Moon. He also speaks to the why the image of the dragon, as he describes it as a serpent merged with an eagle, is especially apt in understanding the powerful symbolism at play here.

Agrippa encourages us to understand the head as holding the nature of Jupiter, regal and heavenly. It is a symbol of good fortune, intelligence, and blessings. The head represents the North Node, a place where the Moon is "swallowed" by the Sun. The head is often symbolic of the intellect and of our 'higher' qualities as human beings. It is through mind that we reach enlightenment, discernment, and tap into the power of our free will and choice. It is the mind itself that we look to for guidance on all things from morality, goodness, and success. It is a symbol of rationality, inspiration, and brilliance.

For the ancient Egyptians, the dragon held special importance, as the carrier of our wishes, to ensure they went to the right divinity, who could fulfill the request. The wish has the added element of fire, facilitating its manifestation. Agrippa notes the special beauty attributed to a dragon's skin in its vibrant color and mythic appeal.

But Agrippa considered the tail of the dragon had the energy of Saturn, Mars, or an eclipsed Moon. Consider the nature of these energies for a moment. Saturn is known for karma or challenges. Mars can be an aggravator. And an eclipsed Moon represents closures that can be dramatic at times. The South Node, and its association with the tail, represents a place of elimination and release. The tail is most often found where the anus of the animal is, a point of excretion. The tail might hold another function of protecting an animal's most vulnerable parts when needed, in sleep, in cold, or in times that call for fear. In this way, the South Node brings with it a place of excretion and elimination, of the things we dont want to look at or see within ourselves, and yet, we protect.

In our own understanding of mythologies surrounding the dragon, they are most often depicted as serpents with wings, who most often have breath consisting of fire. They are symbols of great strength and power, and to tame a dragon is a heroic symbol of overcoming one's own demons.

Perhaps we can consider how mastering our own Nodes can be a pathway towards taming the randomness and sometimes ruthless experience of life. We can take what might be unrolling fire and direct it towards the things we wish to manifest and yet, just like the unpredictability of the mythic dragons, also stay open to what could be even better.

Past Lives And The Archetypal Journey

There are a few different ways that we understand past lives. Perhaps if you think about it, you're imagining yourself running in a field as a little girl, and you can feel the wind in your hair. You might be somewhere in Ireland, and that in a past life memory that you may have thought you were Nefertiti or Cleopatra, right? That is one very common past life that many people identify with.

The truth is that these are ultimately what we call archetypal roles, and what that means is that there is a core energy. For example, royalty. There are many different ways that royalty can express itself. Yes, one way is by having a kingdom, or even being the ruler of a small village somewhere, but it can also be a celebrity who can feel like royalty.

It is ultimately not so much about the names that we're looking at. We're looking more at the roles people played, which allows them to feel like they are in touch with what it feels like to hold a particular position now. Some people will have more specific connections. You may envision yourself as a little girl or as a queen of Egypt. Those are valid, but to understand them ultimately as archetypal, as in some way representing some aspect of your understanding of what you learned and where you have been, gives you that much more understanding about how your growth continues from this moment forward.

There are signs that we look at when we understand archetypes. The South Node most powerfully speaks to the most immediate past life that you are working on, or that you're leaving behind and moving away from, and the future life that you are moving towards is represented by the North Node. Each of these placements is in its own sign, and they're always exactly opposite each other on the zodiac wheel. They follow along a spectrum, going from South to North, or Descending and Ascending. But if you think about the sign that a South Node may be in, that represents a very immediate past life for you.

For example, we can look at Aries as an archetype. It has to do with power and initiative and the pioneering spirit, but it also covers some literal careers as well. So we're looking at things like a warrior, an athlete, a soldier, or a police officer. These are all careers that are covered by the archetype of Aries.

However, there are a lot of different ways to be a warrior. You can be a spiritual warrior. You can be a warrior for a cause. You can be a warrior for your creative vision. And then there are some literal too. It is ultimately about understanding the higher spiritual attributes playing out at any given time that are especially relevant.

Certain core experiences will be a part of this as well. To fight the "good fight" and the sense of being a champion. These are all in alignment with the Aries archetypes that we can understand. They might play out in many different career areas, and in many different roles as well. Whether you are a politician or a parent, there are ways in which you can summon that sense of being a true warrior in your own right. Moving yourself diligently in a direction that you feel is righteous and way to go.

The South Node speaks to what is most familiar to you. It can speak to default characteristics or ways of being. There was a time when you knew who you were going to marry at a very young age. Whether you were told as a child and it was arranged for you by your family. Or as a young person you fell in love as a teenager. There was one person for you, and you knew you would be with them for the rest of your life.

There was a time not that long ago where you didn't have a lot of choice work in your career. You would do what your family did. You will live the same life and work on the same farm. You knew the path in front of you was set. You likely never would have been exposed to different cultures, ideas, or ways of living. There wasn't a whole lot of room for variance from that role placed for you to do.

Of course, we always have these exceptions that stand out as iconic examples, but for the most part, people somewhat understood this. They accepted this. I believe that is because there was a time when we were younger as souls. It would take us a hundred lifetimes to understand the divine lesson playing out in a particular environment. We would spend a full lifetime easily in this established path. We would take a hundred lifetimes with the same person to understand the spiritual dynamic contract playing out to resolve any karmic contracts that are there.

I do believe that we are older souls than ever before. What used to take us a hundred years or a hundred lifetimes, we now get in less time, especially in our modern world. It is not that uncommon to be in several major relationships in our lifetime. It is not that uncommon to have several career paths over the course of our lifetime. It is not that uncommon to experience different cultures, interact with people with very different ways of looking at the world, question the different ways of looking at the world, and find your own path. It is normal now to be curious about what you uniquely are meant to do, experiment with different things, choose a path, and then change course and change gears.

The South Node very often plays out in our early life and childhood. We might reflect back and realize that we often "defaulted" into certain patterns or karmic dynamics as young people. The South Node can speak to whomever you knew yourself to be before. But because we are growing, we are ultimately evolving towards the North Node, towards our future.

We are here to more fully embody the energy I call love and wisdom. This is energy of the Divine, bliss, pure love, the beloved, the sacred, and the many other names we have used to describe that indescribable spark of the timeless mystery within us. We are here to more fully embody and allow it to shine forward in all of our moments. What is your unique pathway towards that going to look like? Well, the North Node points the way.

Interpreting The Nodes

The Nodes are of prime importance in prediction. Depending on the system of astrology that you're using, they'll be more important in some systems than others. For example, in Evolutionary Astrology and Esoteric Astrology schools, special importance is placed on the nodes.

The nodes are always directly across from each other. They are on opposite sides of an axis, ultimately on either side of a single spectrum. The north and south nodes are a pair, and to know one is to know the other.

The South Node in a chart represents what we are moving away from in this lifetime. It is what we have our back to, and it represents the most immediate past life we desire to resolve in this life. Conversely, the North Node is the direction in which we desire to move towards during the course of this lifetime. Life will constantly put us in situations where we will be asked to enter areas of life that are covered by the house that the North Node is in, or will ask us to bring forward the qualities of the sign that the North Node is in at the moment of our birth. As part of the mystery, it is here that we can meet the people that we need, have the experiences we need to, be exposed to certain stimuli, and be exposed to certain ideas as part of understanding what promises it was that we made to ourselves before we incarnated,

We might imagine this as a specific scenario: before we incarnate or enter our body, we sit on a cloud with our guardian angels and guides, and we wait for the planets to align just perfectly so that we can take our first breath. In taking that first breath, we become connected to everyone and everything. We have a symbolic connection to all the inner resources that we need in order to fulfill our highest potential in this life.

The North Node speaks to just how it is that we go about evolving, pulling ourselves into the future, healing the past and actually fulfilling those promises that we made to ourselves.

It has been said that the nodes become easier to access the older that we get, and there are some astrological theories that say that you access the North Node more fully after you have your Saturn returned at twenty-eight and a half. There are others who say that you access this energy more fully after you have your Uranus opposition in your early to mid-forties. However, I do think that we can tap into these energies any time. Self-knowledge makes any part of your chart more accessible.

The North Node isn't necessarily happening on a level of consciousness. The planets speak to what we want, why we want it, and how we go about getting it. The planets speak to our conditioning in a larger sense as well. But the Nodes are all happening on a level of karma. They're happening on a level of spirit. So it isn't that we have to do so much. The indications of the Nodes have a way of finding us.

The South Node is what we're moving away from, and because we're moving away from it, any conjunctions to the South node tend to represent resolution, closing karmic ties, and ending of karmic chapters. Sometimes, it represents people leaving situations that end as well.

If you honor the nodes, everything you need is provided for. I very much believe that the sort of last level of manifestation is the physical, and so things sort of start and creation begins on the level of the spirit, and then it goes to the emotion and then mind and then manifests in the physical, as that is the densest and last place of manifestation. You can see more about my exploration of the levels of existence and more in my previous book, *Prayers To The Sky*.

If you honor what's happening in your life on a level of spirit and a level of emotion, then you will find that the material has a way of balancing out. It has a way of taking care of itself.

The Nodes in a sign and in a house are not the same thing, but it is a useful learning technique to see how the correspondences between signs and houses link the two. It is for this reason that the following chapters bring sign and house together as we explore the nodes, one at a time.

As you read the chapters that cover both your house and sign, you can synthesize the information to personalize it to you. Blending the information in the two chapters is part of what we as astrologers do, and it will help you come to an understanding that is unique to your birth chart.

The Nodes Through The Signs

North Node in Aries

With the North Node in Aries, the fist sign of the zodiac, you will be asked to put yourself first in that area of life, as indicated by the house that the North Node resides. You will attract people and experiences that will invite you to cultivate trust in yourself. An overriding conviction in your passion, your creative vision, and your joy will be part of your karmic pathway forward.

This is the sign of breath, and what feels like breathing is what you will likely always feel a pull towards. We normally think of the things that feel like breathing as those which comes most natural, that resonate so deeply that they could be second nature. Not that this activity wouldn't come with challenges, just that within that, there is an awakened curiosity.

Your earliest experiences showed who you wanted to be, usually based on some activity. You will be asked to therefore trust that state of being that you knew was most natural and right for you.

An Aries North Node is about understanding who you really are at your essence, what it is that you really feel, what it is that you really believe about yourself, what your possibilities are, and what really fires you up. When you ask yourself those questions, then you start tapping into that North Node and you start opening that doorway to move yourself towards your positive evolution and your positive growth by honoring the purpose of your incarnation.

The South Node in Libra can bring with it an over-identification with one's partners and mixed feelings about that. It might be that there is a sense of no individual identity because your partner outshines you, either by being more successful or by garnering more attention. Perhaps there is a fear of this, so you choose partners in early life where there are significant imbalances, so as to be seen as the "better catch."

Possible roles in a past life include guidance counsellor, art dealer, aesthetician, stylist, or a job in human resources. Given the symbolism of scales and needing to find a balanced perspective, roles like a judge or a referee, that require you to consider various possibilities and then make a call, may be familiar roles.

Aries asks for passion, presence, and single-minded dedication. When you bring forward qualities of self-confidence, a pioneering spirit, a willingness to go for the adrenaline rush, and the drive to go your own way, you are able to tap into the best of what your North Node promises.

North Node in Taurus

For the Taurus North Node, your relationship to money, how you understand money, and resolving any money issues will be important. People with a North Node in Taurus might at some point end up working as bill collectors or in credit operations, because it's that type of experience that will make them really confront how emotional an issue money can be. That in turn will help them understand what money is going to mean in this life and what they are putting out in the world, which will determine what they're getting back.

Taurus is an energy of the connoisseur, and while developing the five senses and an appreciation for the finer things will not come naturally, it is the pathway towards finding a greater sense of fulfillment in this life.

Buddha was Taurus–like, and his teachings of presence as the route to enlightenment embody the higher understanding of this sign. For you, moving away from obsessive thoughts and unneeded complications and towards a simpler, more direct way of being in the world is when you begin to understand the higher drive of the soul in this lifetime.

When your North Node is in the sign of Taurus, then you've got your South Node in the sign of Scorpio.

The Scorpio South Node is among the most intense and misunderstood placements. On an emotional level, you are encouraged not to let anybody have any power over you—power in many senses of the word, but especially where it comes to financial power.

Now, Scorpio's energy in its highest understanding is a force of transformation, but in its lowest understanding it can be manipulative, it can be obsessive, and you end up perpetrating those emotions, or some of your actions, however unconscious, end up creating those feelings. A South Node in Scorpio will encourage you to be ever mindful of how you are using this very powerful emotional energy.

Some possible past life roles could include therapist, psychiatrist, detective, market analyst, researcher, financial advisor, or even a pharmacist or surgeon.

The North Node is what we desire to heal, so with this energy, life is going to be about healing any obsession, and about moving away from being the type of person who would be manipulative. Obsessions are about being in a whole other energy space and about not being totally present, and so, slowly coming into the moment and slowly coming into the present experience is what the energy of Taurus promises.

North Node in Gemini

The North Node in the sign of Gemini invites the development of spontaneity. Finding your voice, learning to express yourself in the moment, and being free spirited in the expression. You will be encouraged to improvise ideas, and then through being stimulated by that idea, allow your creativity to spark.

Your inclination towards learning from your past life will help you as you learn to juggle many activities at the same time, or multitask, and ultimately, it is this ability that will put you in another energy space that will help you evolve, grow, and see things within yourself that will help you develop the skills that you need. Furthermore, you will attract people that will help you adapt these skills you have learned so that you can use them in different types of situations. It is all part of really honoring the purpose of your incarnation, which is to develop your perception, to think for yourself and to honor your voice.

With the Gemini North Node, comes the Sagittarius South Node. Life may ask you to move away from just a very limited way of understanding the highest principles and philosophies, and from an understanding of the world that is based ultimately on separation and meta principles that are limited. The South Node in Sagittarius invites you to be present in the moment and being open to know more.

However, with the Sagittarius energy, it is important not to think that you know the truth and not to fall into that energy where you think that you know what the truth is, especially when it is a political, philosophical or religious truth.

Possible past life career or life paths might have included roles as a preacher, priest, lawyer, explorer, traveller, public relations advisor, or even a coach or other figure who was encouraging and inspiring others around them.

There is real complexity in the world, but that can be part of its beauty. Self awareness and spiritual understanding is often right in front of you, in the people and in the conversations you might have. Much of our reality is found in perception. You will be asked to develop your mind and choose perceptions that will empower you and make your life better.

North Node in Cancer

The sign of Cancer has to do with learning through emotions and feelings. It is about separating fear from intuition. There's a powerful sensitivity with the sign of Cancer, so if you have the North Node in Cancer, life is going to throw you into situations where you have to develop your intuition. Where you have to acknowledge your fear and understand how fear is perhaps guiding some of your instincts. This energy may make you feel very vulnerable, but you can actually use that to your advantage.

If your North Node is in the sign of Cancer, then you are likely pouring this energy out in its highest manifestation by directing the sensitivity to your advantage and using it to be of greater service in the world. It has to do with understanding that ultimately all these different experiences that you have and all these different strong emotions that can be felt by a person are there as a gift, and that you are responsible for that gift and for using it wisely.

When the North Node is in a water sign, it tends to denote a very strong connection with the spirit, so things will manifest on a spiritual level before they move to the level of emotion. The North Node in the sign of Cancer is developing that emotion as part of pushing your evolution along.

If you have got your North Node in the sign of Cancer, then your South Node will be in the sign of Capricorn. Capricorn understands that anything that is worth having is worth working towards, and it will actually commit to the plan and the process to see a goal through. When the South Node is in the sign of Capricorn, it's about moving away from any workaholic type of energy and work for its own sake, or working and achieving as a way of feeling better about yourself instead of truly feeling good just for being you. It's also about understanding materialism in its proper place and understanding the material realm.

In early life, tendencies towards taking on too much responsibility can present itself. Possible past life career choices or roles might have included a boss or authority figure, someone who took on responsibility within a family as the elder, or as a leader of an organization. A manager or business consultant who helped others achieve the success you had might have been a natural.

Ultimately, life is going to take on a greater depth and greater meaning for you, and you're going to meet the people that you need to fill your karmic contracts and to do the things that your soul desires to do in this lifetime. However, you first have to figure out what you really feel and where maybe fear has been motivating some of your actions. You'll be guided to instead choose genuine intuition, rooted in a connection that we all have to each other on the most basic of levels, understanding that we all here at this time as one human family, and that is a rewarding understanding to have.

North Node in Leo

Leo represents life and the acknowledgment that there is something within you that is worthy of shining and being seen. It's also about connecting to that part of you. The sign of Leo rules the heart and it has to do with what lights up your heart as well, so it's taking what is a joy for you, what's fun for you, and finding a way to just share that and know that you're worthy of being acknowledged and seen for that in the world.

With the South Node in the sign of Aquarius, over-identifying with a group is likely, especially in early life. There is a need to be careful that you are not overly concerned with fitting in, or being like others in order to feel a part of something, for its own sake. Belonging that is rooted in genuine similarities is more rewarding, but might not come as easily. Aquarius is also the sign of eccentricity. There is the likelihood of performative rebellion, that is being eccentric just for the novelty or shock value, rather than from a genuine, inner truth. It is wearing rebellion rather than being truly independent and self-trusting.

The South Node in the sign of Aquarius can find overidentification with contrary or adversarial perspectives simply for their argumentative opportunities rather than sincere belief. Being so overcommitted to an ideology that you become unable to see any other perspective, believing that nothing else matters other than this idea or viewpoint. True rebellion is being true to yourself because so few people do it.

From a past life perspective, a person with an Aquarian South Node might have memories of lives as an outcast, rebel, scientist, inventor, social worker, astronomer, astrologer, or alchemist.

The movement away from the South Node towards the North Node is an understanding deep within the soul that if you're ever really going to do what it is that you desire to do in this life, you're going to have to stop listening to other people and stop thinking about what a group of people might think, and instead go in the direction of what your heart feels called to do. If you do that, then you're going to find yourself reaching a flow in life. It doesn't mean that the work is any less, but life will start to feel a little easier when you're honoring the purpose of the incarnation. Everything that you need on a material level will be provided because you're honoring the ultimate purpose of this lifetime, which is to grow spiritually, to learn what you need, and to move towards greater love and greater wisdom.

The Leo North Node asks you to embrace your most creative and instinctual self. It asks you to take a gamble on life with your creative energy and creative vision. The more outlandish the passion, the more likely it is to pay off.

North Node in Virgo

In our spiritual evolution, the sign of Virgo has to do with expertise. It has to do with putting in your 10,000 hours, doing something often and long enough to achieve mastery and be able to consider yourself an expert at it, and, ultimately, the highest understanding of Virgo is that there is a part of you that wants to know what the North Node is; there's a part of you that is aiming to be really good at least one thing over the course of this life, even if it's only a very private and personal recognition of your expertise, and then, as a result of the work and the hours that you've put in, garnering a sense of self-respect and self-understanding.

As a result, when you've got your North Node in the sign of Virgo, you are going to be asked to become good at something, to stick to a path long enough and really to pay attention to details, as well to consider how you're utilizing the smallest moments of your day and of your life towards building a version of yourself that you can be proud of. You're going to be asked to consider also the smallest moments and what their consequences are in the bigger picture. Life is going to ask you to focus and to consider the consequences of the smallest details, and in paying attention to those details, you'll be able to really understand how you are made better as a result of your cultivating a sense of attention to those details to the smallest moments of life.

With this placement comes the South Node in the sign of Pisces. With the Pisces South Node, connection to a past life might have felt especially immediate. Whether it was through extremely vivid dreams, or an early environment that encouraged such awareness. An exceptional ability or strong affinity towards art or music might have been there in childhood.

Possible past life roles might have included being involved with films, whether in front or behind the camera, a photographer, a spiritualist or faith leader, an artist or musician, a monk, a nun, a hospice worker, or even a social worker where you expressed notable compassion.

Remember, the North Node is not necessarily happening on a level of consciousness. It has to do with what's happening on a level of spirit or soul. What's happening on a level of matter is the final manifestation of the things that started in spirit, then became emotion, then manifested to the mind and intellect and finally broke through on the level of matter.

Those with the North Node in the sign of Virgo will have to invest time into developing a relationship with the physical body. Sometimes you will manifest little aches and pains or other health issues so that you can learn some of these sacred lessons. You can learn to pay attention to the details. Just what are you eating? What are you digesting? Not only in terms of your food, but also in terms of what's coming in, in terms of the stimulation of intellectual ideas and all that jazz. But detailed jazz.

Since it is in the pursuit of well-being that you might make key karmic connections, you might find special relationships with those who are in the medical or health professions. And so, by displaying physical symptoms, you might be promoted to connect with these very people. So if you are presenting with symptoms that you need help with, it's that much more important to reach out and get the professional medical care you need.

There's also an understanding here that when you start manifesting these little things, it is about considering the whole picture—not just what you're doing, but also what you are feeling. What's happening on the level of spirit that's trying to get your attention? You might be asked to explore and consider different types of health modalities or traditional medicines.

Practices that allow you to experience a greater sense of well-being within your own body can serve as a starting point towards taking ownership for the preciousness that is each day.

North Node in Libra

The North Node leads us to manifest the higher end of the energy represented in the sign. With the North Node in the sign of Libra, trying to attract partners, cultivating the skill of compromise, and having a sounding board will encourage you to take action in a way that will reflect well on others. You will attract experiences that help you understand the value of considering different perspectives. You will be encouraged to cultivate a spirit of diplomacy and a more gracious approach in your interactions.

Socrates spoke about the difference between Earthly Aphrodite and Celestial Aphrodite. I think of Taurus as relaxing on the beach and bathing in the warmth of Earthly Aphrodite due to its possessiveness of Venus's energy during the day. (For more on day and night associations, see my book *Astrology Realized*).

Celestial Aphrodite has to do with understanding the balanced nuance of beauty in its highest form and the contrast the stars present against the night sky. The beauty of ideas, of philosophies, of architectures are eternally defined as Venus shimmers gracefully across the midnight canvas like a sparkly chariot carrying the dreams of lovers. It is here that beauty is based on ideas of your own choosing and on more enlightened concepts.

With this placement comes a South Node in Aries. In early life, there might have been a feeling of needing to fight in some way. Early experiences might have reinforced the need to survive, to act instinctually, and as part of this, impulsive tendencies might have predominated. Exaggerated or childish displays of behavior in order to do things your own way might have been notably rewarded. This can sometimes indicate that the "terrible twos" stage of development stretched out well into the teens or beyond.

This may all sound very daunting, but it takes a determined soul to assert its right to be here in this life, to be heard, to be seen. Knowing that your own needs are worth being met is likely a feeling you came into this life with. Even in times of wavering self-worth or feelings of insecurity, you know how to hold your head high, especially when it takes guts. Reckless risk taking can give way to calculated moves that move you closer to your higher objectives.

With the South Node in Aries, you are moving away from being a law unto yourself. You're moving away from an understanding that you are all that matters, that there is no one other than yourself, and that your most immediate passion is the thing that life is all about. By moving towards a level of understanding other viewpoints, of taking into account all the various perspectives before you act, you move your life and growth forward. Sometimes it takes really having to stretch yourself to find middle ground with another person.

Possible past life roles might have included a pioneer, an entrepreneur, an athlete, firefighter or law enforcement officer. Emergency medicine, for its high-adrenaline, high-stakes environment might have also been a space of familiarity. Drumming or another artistic medium that includes a strong physical application might have also driven you on the path your soul once walked.

Sometimes, it takes skill and commitment to say to yourself, "I'm going to stop and take a breath before I act. I'm going to wait a moment and I'm going to ask somebody before I do something that I feel like I've really really got to do, especially when I think that that action could be taken as aggression." With the North Node in the sign of Libra, this is the work you are asked to do.

The journey away from self-centeredness or thinking that life is just about you, and instead moving towards sharing and cooperation is where the soul grows and shines in this lifetime. You know on a soul level that it's good for you to learn how to get along with other people, to consider their feelings, and as a result, you are made better through understanding their perspective on the world. Doing this and finding a happy medium allows you to move, not only towards greater love or appreciation with that person, but also towards greater wisdom as well.

North Node in Scorpio

Scorpio energy is considered especially intense, but that is because it represents a full immersion in life, from all of its feelings, desires, its ugliness, but also the promise of change. It covers psychoanalysis and the life-death-rebirth cycle. At some point in life, the opportunity to undergo a process of therapy will likely arise. Whether it is in a formalized setting working with a therapist, or through an interest in self-help and personal exploration, it is the pursuit of self-knowledge that lends itself to a start afresh.

Scorpio has been understood as being associated with elimination, with what you consciously let go and what you consciously keep. It is realizing that the way that you are going to make progress and move forward is through letting go of what you don't need, of what you have fully used, or has served its purpose. Sometimes this will be done very consciously, smoothly and easily. Other times, this will be undergone through resistance, with reluctance to accept the change.

Sometimes it is relationships or people, and sometimes situations, that ask for this process of self-honesty, authenticity, and transformation. Where people and situations can evolve with us, those bonds are made that much stronger. Where it is that they can't, we might be asked to move forward.

Trust issues can arise, with the larger opportunity of learning to trust others. The larger lesson is to know that whatever may happen with others in your life, as long as you have what is true and real within, you will be all right. Allowing yourself to be vulnerable to others, sharing of yourself more deeply and emotionally, are ways the Scorpio North Node gains power and purpose in this lifetime. Trust that other people will be kind with you if you show them the part of yourself that you don't really like to share, or that you don't like seeing.

A North Node in Scorpio will bring with it a South Node in Taurus. Larger lessons of self worth might be especially pronounced. There was possibly the message of "not being enough," for usually superficial reasons. There might have been messages that led to an insecurity around your inherent worthiness, or your lovability. The opportunity is to move towards the North Node, that reminds you that what makes you most worthy and most beautiful is not about the superficial factors, but what lies at the core of you.

A Taurus South Node might have an especially strong appetite as a child, enjoying food for the sensual delight of it. Overdoing this practice might be a part of the early life, but so is the opportunity to learn through the five senses, and using them towards your higher aims.

Possible past life roles might have included chef, for the ability to cultivate taste. The Taurus sign might have manifested as a past life career in banking, or the management of money. Connoisseurs of all kinds can be found with this energy, including in wine, art, and chocolate. Jeweler, makeup artist and clothing designer for the Venusian connection of this sign. Finally, as an energy of the earth, anything from an environmentalist to a natural magic partitioner might be familiar roles for your soul. An especially distinct voice, wether as a speaker or singer, might have presented opportunities. Some of these unique vocal qualities may still be present intros lifetime.

Scorpio encourages you to see the beauty, love and wisdom in what is normally rejected, in what's considered low, what we hide or what is taboo. It is an energy of seeing all the underlying motivations and all the manipulations that take place, whether we are conscious of them or not. So sometimes, for example, with a North Node in the sign of Scorpio, you are one who is going to attract people who tend to be rather intense or you will bring forward qualities of intensity. Also, with the North Node in the sign of Scorpio, you will be asked to be a force of transformation and a force of evolution, a force that allows yourself and other people to rise from the ashes, which is what the Scorpio vibration is all about.

Conclusively, with a North Node in the sign of Scorpio, the whole idea of life-death-rebirth becomes especially pronounced and at least once in a lifetime, people with this aspect in the chart will go through a major process of rebirth by getting rid of all that they don't need that gets in the way of them fully stepping into the embodiment of love and wisdom that we are all moving towards, individually and collectively as well.

North Node in Sagittarius

Sagittarius energy is generally thought of as being independent and restless. Enthusiasm is what helps give this otherwise listless energy focus and direction. Knowing that you are moving towards something that lights you up, something that gives you joy, or simply an adventure you look forward to, will allow you to tap into some of the best energy of this placement. Sagittarius as your North Node is your ticket to trust what is fun for you and trust what lights you up, because that is where most of your important spiritual lessons are going to come from.

Life might ask you to undertake a pilgrimage at least once in your lifetime, for your own personal and spiritual good, and for a sense of your own happiness. You might also find yourself attracted to different places, so that you participate in the rite of pilgrimage more than once. This might be conscious and within the confines of a specific tradition. So, you might find yourself visiting a widely recognized holy site. Or perhaps, your chosen pilgrimage will be more eclectic, representing either a personal or modern religious movement. Undertaking this pilgrimage is going to help you to be happier in the world. It serves as an invitation to get honest with yourself about what you really need to be happy and to feel a greater sense of enthusiasm for your life. The answers you find will stay with you and become a key part of your alignment with love and wisdom.

When you have your North Node in Sagittarius, you'll find your South Node directly opposite in Gemini. This energy can go in two distinct directions. A gift of gab and natural ability to connect and communicate might be recognized at an early age. But this placement can also go to the other extreme, with early life challenges with speech or with learning.

Ensuring that you are sharing from a place of genuine, though subjective, truth, and appreciating how powerful your message can be, can help you move away from talking for its own sake and towards having something meaningful to say.

Possible past life environments might have included a job within the media, perhaps as a journalist or editor. Whether in print, radio, or television, wherever it is that information is shared, or where people are talking, are likely familiar stomping grounds. A grade school teacher or child education specialist might have been career paths. An engineer or computer programer utilizes the Air qualities of this sign. And a way with words might have lent itself to a stenographer or video gamer, for engaging hand-eye coordination might have been a past life natural knack.

The Sagittarius North Node helps you cultivate a special adaptability, being able to find home wherever you go, and to see yourself in diverse types of people. Your journey towards greater love and greater wisdom will have you seeing the entire world as a space of spiritual evolution.

North Node in Capricorn

Capricorn's energy brings a sense of self-respect that comes from having a vision or a goal and sticking to the process long enough to see it come to fruition. There's a certain level of pride in one's self that comes from knowing that you honored the physical plane and the process of manifestation. You stuck to a plan, remained nimble where needed, but through perseverance reap the rewards.

Capricornian energy encourages the appreciation of the self-worth, self-understanding and self-assurance that comes from becoming an authority figure. Through sheer resolve of following the steps needed and seeing it through no matter how long it takes, you may step into roles of greater responsibility and greater ascendency over the course of your lifetime. Bringing an energy of ambition and action, towards the realization of a goal, can bring with it a constant reminder of the legacy you are creating in all your moments.

Capricorn's energy asks us to dissociate from an idea of a day job which allows us to meet our current needs. Instead, we are invited to raise our vision. We are asked to fit whatever we are doing today into this vision and trust that some sense of our daily process will be a part of our consistent movement towards a larger ambition. Finding yourself naturally drawn to success will likely be a low reveal, rarely connected to the vision in your early life of what success means. In this way, the definition of success itself is something that evolves slowly and meaningfully over the course of one's lifetime.

The symbol of Capricorn is found in the mountain goat. Long considered a symbol of virility and independence, a North Node placed in this sign holds special blessings of fruition and fertility. This might not be in a physical sense, for that you'd have to consider other indications of children in the natal chart. This can also be the ability to multiply opportunity and ideas so they carry momentum and are able to be greater than they were before. The independent spirt shows us our ability to take initiative and trust the vision of what we hope to manifest.

A North Node in Capricorn means that your South Node will be in the sign of Cancer. Cancer brings with it heightened feelings, especially an early life, where we might confuse our fears for our instincts or vice versa. There might be especially strong attachments to the maternal figure in one's life. This placement can also indicate complicated feelings around how we were mothered, but also brings with it the opportunity to understand the generational memories we carry more deeply.

A strong sense of connection to one's ancestors may display itself by being instinctually called to certain paths or characteristics, whether or not you knew this person personally. A physical resemblance to one of our ancestors might be uncanny to the elders in the life, who may remark on how much the facial characteristics resemble someone from long ago.

The early life can also bring with it a notable, strong appetite, especially for foods that are heavy in nature, providing grounding through grains or carbohydrates. Or perhaps unusual food preferences or allergies might be present. These can sometimes be outgrown as the person grows older. At birth, the face or eyes might be uncharacteristically round for your family line.

Heightened sensitivity to the world around you can encourage you to eventually develop "tough skin," though you learn to shine when you stay connected to your more caring side. Healthy forms of care, especially for others, might be hard won lessons that come slowly, but surely.

The Cancer sign's strong association with home might indicate past life roles as a real estate agent, interior home designer, or even homemaker. The hold this sign has on the past can also speak to past life experiences with antiques or archives. Food as nurturance can speak to roles as a chef, baker, nutritionist, or caterer.

The Cancer/Capricorn axis encourages us to move away from simple familiarity and towards responsibility. Away from resting our potential on who we are, and instead identifying more strongly with what we do. When the actions are rooted in reverence for the past, yet focused on what you can do today to create your future reality, is when you are able to make the most of this North Node.

North Node in Aquarius

Aquarius rules what we call the Age of Enlightenment, coinciding with the discovery of the modern ruling planet of Aquarius, Uranus. Historically, this brought with it the Scientific Revolution, which moved us to what we called a Cartesian split, a separation of matter from spirit. Since we separated matter from spirit, we've been able to recognize equality right across the board for all types of people, regardless of gender, race, or ability. We are able to recognize the great equalizing factor in all of us when rooted in intellect.

With an Aquarius North Node, we are asked to understand this separation and its highest sense so we can bring a spirit of equality in all that we do. We are asked to cultivate our intellect, and through the discernment of a variety of ways of thinking, we find our own unique ways of putting those ideas together. It is in bringing together previously unconnected ideas that a truly unique contribution can be made. One that is creative, even revolutionary, in nature.

Aquarius is often associated with groups, but as an energy holds a strong independent spirit. It is therefore inner authority that is relied on above the dictates of tradition or hierarchy. The egalitarian nature of this sign recognizes us all as equal, but the contradiction of this sign also believes that we are all special. The Aquarian North Node in particular will ask that we embrace and trust those things that make us unique and stay true to them.

Recognition of one's specialness is a necessary condition towards self-trust and self-reliance. The emphasis on self ultimately allows that much more to be brought to others, especially within group dynamics. The belief that "we are all equal because are all special" is part of how growth towards a more enlightened self is found.

Aquarius is also connected to the New Age because it creates a bridge between science and art, empirical facts and imaginative visions. With its ancient ruler Saturn long considered a symbol of transition, and its modern ruler Uranus speaking to futuristic change, the juxtaposition will normally find an emphasis between one urge over the other. With an Aquarian North Node you are asked to look ahead and to think about the future more expansively. At the same time, the desire to build something solid with traditional approval presents differing motivations you are asked to navigate.

An Aquarian North Node will come with a South Node in the sign of Leo. Leo is the sign of the king, and if you think about monarchs, much of their assertion of validity rests in their specialness. There is only one of them, whether by birthright or ranking. Where Aquarius moves towards dismantling hierarchies, Leo sits on top of it.

With a Leo South Node you instinctively knew from a very young age that you are special in some way. Whether you are the king or queen of your family, or take an easy role of leadership, the early life affirms a sense of greatness within. This might sometimes come with advantages and rewards. The early life might involve special attention or opportunities to shine.

However, an early message around attention being equal to love can bring an exaggerated desire for public esteem. If any attention is good, then particularly dramatic statements that bring attention, regardless of how it might be judged, can still become symbolic of love. These are the children with an especially notable "terrible twos" phase. This phase of development moves the child away from being the center of the Universe to those around them and asks them to develop empathy and consideration of others. A journey that is easier for some children than others.

Rooting the confidence of eternal qualities with kindness and heart-centered behaviors that allow an overall positive self-assessment is the first step towards raising the energy of the Leo South Node and moving it forward. The life path will necessarily ask to continuously move away from being overly concerned with the self, and instead find a renewed sense by giving generously to others for its own sake. An overly generous nature in childhood, as a way to make others love you, can progress to healthy ways of giving to others from a place that has more than enough genuine love and warmth to give.

Past life roles might include memories of being royalty with a penchant towards romance. Perhaps a notable king like Henry VIII, or a ruler like Cleopatra. Or maybe a figure more anonymous to history, but respected nonetheless. A theatrical Vaudeville performer or film actor tap into the charismatic performance qualities of the Leo South Node. Comedians often enjoy the power to invoke a hearty laugh in others. Outside of performance, this is also the sign of being a child or enjoying the company of children, and this placement can indicate a special fondness for the more playful ways of moving through the world. Sales might be one of the first jobs you find in this lifetime, with heightened charisma proving to be influential on others.

The potential of the Aquarian North Node is to bring a truly visionary perspective that ultimately brings people together. The creativity of the past can give way to a purposeful imagination that creates meaningful change within the collective.

North Node in Pisces

Pisces is the energy of communion, compassion and forgiveness. It is submerged in the collective unconscious, swimming through everyone and everything. The North Node in Pisces will be called to connect with Source in one way or another. Whether through the cultivation of music or meditation, or bringing an instinctive, creative perspective. This where it is that when you move beyond intellect and towards the immersion of life, you begin to align with the higher qualities of the Pisces North Node.

The Pisces North Node will encourage you to move in the direction of your own evolution through energy and the energetic spaces you dwell in, even if you can't intellectualize it or verbalize it. This means that you are learning to trust the part of you that doesn't need to understand or have all the information and details. It is the ability to flow though your experiences that allows you to excel within them.

Compassion is a key characteristic for Pisces. When you allow yourself to be immersed in energy itself, you cannot help but feel the energetic state of others. This may not always be a conscious effort. Rather, a natural ability to "pick up" the mood of the person near you, or the room you enter, allows you to make the most of it, for spiritual, personal, or professional gain. The ability to tap into a more compassionate spirit consciously is there, and is recommended to cultivate. If this energy isn't engaged in consciously, you might find yourself attracting experiences where you have to forgive people to cultivate compassion. People may behave in ways that will make it difficult to be compassionate to them, and yet part of the life path may ask you to do just that.

Joseph Campbell famously said, "Follow your bliss." This is a guiding mantra for the person with a Pisces North Node. This placement encourages trust in what feels right to you energetically, whether or not it makes intellectual sense. It blesses us with the greatest progress when we approach what we do from a meditative state; completely immersed, and in an altered state of consciousness, where stream of creation and productivity is able to come forward naturally.

This is also the strength of the mystic. To allow oneself to be in the presence of the Divine might require shifting perspectives in order to allow the awareness to come in. Cultivating ways to enter an altered state of consciousness while maintaining a feeling of safety is a pathway towards powerful, life-defining, and mystical experiences that can dramatically alter the life path at key moments.

The Pisces North Node will always accompanied by a South Node in Virgo. Virgo is notoriously the energy of details, and is sometimes accused of being nit-picky. Whether it arises from a desire to understand or the desire to control, a need for an abundance of information can stall action. Over-perfectionism can be an area that hides deep insecurity of not being good enough. This can make one too anxious to take any action, which in and of itself could help improve circumstances.

The early life likely held experiences that emphasized the need pay attention to minute details, in a way that created distress. An obsessive need to practice, whether it came from within or was demanded by the first caregivers, might have lent itself to an exceptional display of well earned skill in at least one area. An obsessive need for cleanliness might have been emphasized, and early habits might have been too harsh on the skin, perhaps lending themselves to problems that require healing in later life. This is one placement that can indicate notable or severe acne the early timid teens, that is outgrown once adulthood is entered.

A Virgo South Node might also indicate an especially sensitive digestive system in early life, especially in childhood, with a focus paid on the eating habits. Food enjoyed by others in the early family environment might have had times of being intolerable. The body's rejection of being nurtured might have been a source of distress. However, as the person with this placement grows, they might find an intuitive approach to eating to be especially helpful. Aligning food choices with higher, spiritual principals of compassion or spiritual meaning help create amore stable ability to nurture the self.

Past life roles might have included a connection to health care. A dietician, nutritionist, health care aide, or nurse might have been especially suited to your abilities, along with a family physician or general medical practitioner. These roles would bring forward the value of the small acts of care that add up to positive changes that the sign of Virgo is known for. This attentiveness to care might have been directed towards small animals and pets, so a natural penchant towards veterinary care might have been present. This sign has a reputation for cleanliness, and past life roles as a housekeeper, cleaner, or homemaker who brought notable attention to detail might have factored in. The Mercurial rulership of this sign might also speak to a past life or childhood penchant towards computer technologies or copywriting.

Wherever the North Node is, you're asked to go above and beyond, to a higher and more enlightened understanding of this energy. The sign of Pisces connects to the experience of being swept up in spirit itself, moving beyond simple enlightenment towards a lighter, yet more immersive state of being. The Pisces North Node asks that we move away from understanding or needing to know, and instead to feel so deeply that you can't help but glimpse the truth of life, which is that elusive oneness that we all crave. In this way, this lifetime promises that this life will be fully lived, with all your feelings and emotions ultimately pointing the way to genuine compassion that can't help but also be extended to the self.

The Nodes Through
The Houses

North Node in The 1st House

The 1st House and its association with the Ascendant represents our first breath, instinct to life, and speaks to our first and most immediate gut reaction. Breath itself represents inspiration in its most literal sense, as it is breath that evokes spirit into the body itself. This first place of the chart becomes the place where we identify most strongly. It is the things that matter to us first and foremost that are indicated.

The 1st House North Node will ask you to bring a focus on your own desires in this lifetime. In addition, it invites you to be aware of what it is that brings inspiration, how and by what you are most immediately inspired, and how you understand yourself at your innermost essence. If it matters to you, it matters. Integrating this life lesson is part of how the soul grows most.

Much of this life will lead you towards honoring your own instincts and impulses, honoring what you feel and not only what you need. It is about honoring who you believe yourself to be.

There might be a strong sense of destiny with this placement, which is strengthened the closer the North Node lies to the Ascendant (AC). A strong sense of who you are and an emphasis of defining yourself solely based on your own presence and inspiration, and not based on association with others, can be indicated.

If you have your North Node in the 1st House, then your South Node will be in the 7th House. The South Node tends to manifest most in our earlier life, and it represents our most immediate past life that we desire to resolve and move away from in this life. I've found one of two scenarios are most possible with the South Node in the 7th House.

The first scenario is that you will find that person that you're meant to be with, and that you then might enter a major relationship with this person or perhaps formally marry early in life. Once you know you have a partnership locked in, there is no longer any need to consider the pursuit of a partner. Your relationship might have come together with ease, and is your easiest place to be, so now you can focus more fully on yourself and your own inspiration for the things that matter to you.

In the second scenario, one may find that life invites them to spend time on their own and to place focus and importance on their own perspective. To maintain a very strong sense of self and of one's own identity, they may resist committing to long term partnerships. Even within relationships, they might find that life continues to ask for a strong spirit of independence with plenty of time and space to cultivate the individual path. It is also possible that the early life brings partners who detract from the path of one's choosing, and relationships can feel like they take too much energy until a healthy balance is cultivated between the actions of another and the individual prompt of the soul.

The great gift of the North Node in the 1st House is that it brings with it the potential to excel in this life for the things that matter most to you.

North Node in The 2nd House

The North Node in the 2nd House, very simply put, is going put one continuously in a position where the self has to provide for itself through its own efforts. It is where steps must be take to meet the needs of self and the practical needs of the people to whom there is responsibility. It is in the process of providing for the self and earning money that key soul contracts are fulfilled. Those that might facilitate some of our most important growth will be presented in these environments. Because of this need operating on a level of soul, opportunities to make money will always be there.

This placement creates confidence that money making opportunities will always be there, and they certainly will.

Because earning an income is tied to the true intention of this lifetime, the spiritual development of the soul, opportunities are sure to be there when needed. It is as if the Universe knows that it will be through working and earning your own money that you are going to meet the people you need. The experiences needed to fulfill the karmic contracts you made to the self and to others are here. It's also a place where karmic blessings are most readily received.

When a natal planet conjuncts the North Node in the 2nd House, people who in some way exemplify the archetype of that planet are likely to be drawn in at different points in the lifetime. They help create greater prosperity and greater opportunity. For example, Jupiter conjunct a 2nd House North Node holds the knack of attracting particularly boisterous or philosophical types. This can also indicate prosperity is found through Jupitarian endeavors. (For much more on this, note the next section in this book dedicated to planets in aspect to the Nodes.)

One's relationship with money and prosperity itself is covered here. There will likely be many opportunities to further examine and evolve abundance in one's life. The relationship and beliefs around money will be examined at some point in the lifetime. Healing any issues that get in the way of prosperity may be part of the spiritual lessons that present themselves. There can also be the development of a more enlightened perspective on prosperity defined in deeply personal, spiritually grounded ways.

Possessions are found in the 2nd House, and acquiring deeply meaningful, spiritually relevant possessions will form part of the pursuit of this lifetime. Keeping possessions in their proper place, so you see them as symbolic rather than literally valuable, is part of the path of the cultivation of wisdom.

Self-esteem and self-love can be found in the 2nd House. The opportunity to constantly move towards more empowered states of self-value will show up though experiences and people.

The North Node in the 2nd House will naturally connect with a South Node in the 8th House. The 8th House is considered especially intense, holding issues of trust and power struggles. The early life might have demonstrated these characteristics, especially in relation to money. These early experiences likely fortified the need to be self sufficient that much more.

The 2nd House North Node encourages you to move away from sharing, being dependent, or relying on others, whether that be people or institutions, and towards your own power and your own independence. This might play out financially or emotionally. The blessing is the opportunity to step into a genuine sense of knowing what healthy and empowered self-love is.

North Node in The 3rd House

The North Node in the 3rd house encourages the development of one's voice, spiritualizing perceptions, and the cultivation of one's mind. The North Node in the 3rd house will also ask you to learn and develop your skills to continue to grow, constantly improving and learning. You will be asked to find out what your voice is in this lifetime, how it is that you will share it, and how it is that you are going to express yourself.

Your position within your family in terms of those who are considered equal to you, as in your relations with siblings and cousins, may be an area that constantly asks for your attention. Your responsibilities to these types of people in your life, how you communicate with these people, what role these people are going to play in your life, and how these people will bless your life, especially when it looks like the opposite is happening, will be part of the exploration of this lifetime.

Especially strong karmic bonds can be present with siblings, cousins, and neighbors. These people represent karmic blessings, and in many ways, can open up opportunities to you. A calling to contribute more locally, as in your immediate community, might present itself. Running a local food drive or running for a position on the condo board might be some ways to stay involved. It is in participation in these endeavors that karmic contracts are fulfilled and great personal and spiritual growth is found.

The North Node in the 3rd house will accompany a South Node in the 9th house. The South Node in the 9th house invites movement away from being self-righteous and overly ideological. It invites movement away from looking at the world from a rigid perspective, or a limited philosophical perspective. It invites moving away from understanding the world simply through what you've been told it to be.

With a South Node in the 9th house, I have found two possible scenarios, each representing an extreme. It is usually the case that higher education comes very easily. It can feel natural to pursue higher education and those opportunities seem to come naturally. Higher education can also speak to philosophical ideas, concepts or theories, what it means to be human and not purely instinctual, thinking about the meaning of life and of higher ways of looking at the world. Therefore, any areas or institutions that deal with such things like universities, legal institutions, political institutions will show up, and it can seem almost natural to be there. I will just feel comfortable.

The other scenario is that more formal educational opportunities feel as if they are denied, so that the need to build more practical skills comes together more easily. There might be a rejection of formal institutions, in that early life showed the darker side of these spaces, and so there is a resistance to participating in them.

With the North Node in the 3rd house, you are invited to be in the present moment. It is in that space that we can realize that many truths are highly relative and deeply personal. Once this realization occurs, we can then move to the place of understanding the difference between belief and fact.

North Node in The 4th House

The 4th House is related to home and the past. Everything from creating a safe space for yourself in the world to a home that feels comfortable can be found in this most private part of the chart. Your roots, your culture and its connection to identity, and what that's going to mean on a fundamental level, are all based here. Your ancestors and physical ancestry is found here, including your most immediate ancestors, your parents.

If we look at the 4th House with a deeper significance, the 4th House also has to do with feeling at home, either in your childhood or where you actually live, or the feeling of being home in your own body and in your own skin. It means to truly feel comfortable in a safe space alone, and to know that you would be okay in that space of aloneness. If you feel safe within, you can go in the world that much more. It is the foundations of your life that constantly evoke the journey towards greater love and greater wisdom.

The North Node is in the 4th House accompanies a South Node in the 10th House, and wherever the South Node is, that's what we're moving away from over the course of this lifetime. Therefore, if your South Node is in the 10th House, there is a movement away from simply achieving. Success, accomplishments, or having public status for its own sake. The move is towards a more comfortable inner state of self-acceptance from a perspective of the fulfillment of the soul's promises to itself.

With the South Node in the 10th House, it becomes much less about receiving that recognition or being seen more broadly, and it becomes more about recognizing the value of private moments and the value of having a fortress of solitude. Not needing necessarily to live out loud and live in public, but to find a way to have a sense of yourself and not worrying much about what other people see more publicly.

A 4th House North Node brings a deep connection to the ancestors, and the cultivation of awareness as to how life is continually blessed because of them. This brings that much more purpose and meaning to all moments.

North Node in The 5th House

The 5th house invites deep trust in what passions call the spirit. Acknowledging or figuring out just what your passion is, and then going with it and developing it to its maximal potential, is part of what the life path may ask. The 5th House is sometimes associated with self-employment when it's rooted in a personal sense of joy. Taking the passion seriously becomes important, as its lends to soul fulfillment. It may also provide a connection with greater prosperity. In fact, this placement can indicate going from "rags to riches."

The 5th House also has to do with trusting your instincts and taking a risk, including in activities like gambling. The greatest gamble we might take is in ourselves; our own creativity and instincts. The 5th House has been said to be related with leisure activities and hobbies. Things you like to do in your downtime. It's through doing those things that you are led towards meeting the people and having the experiences needed which ultimately are part of fulfilling some of those promises that you made to yourself before you incarnated.

In modern astrology, the 1st House has come to be known with true love. This represents our changing understanding of love and courtship itself as an ultimately personal and singular endeavor at first. Flirtation and the rush of new feelings that attraction provides can be found here. It's where you have the beginning moments of connecting with another. A North Node placement here can indicate many opportunities to know this "rush" of love in this lifetime. Even the smallest flirtations can facilitate profound spiritual growth and spiritual understanding.

The 5th House is often connected to self-actualization. As illustrated in Maslow's Hierarchy, once the most basic needs are met, what we feel is of most importance evolves and grows. The ultimate aim of the human experience is to be well used for the things you like about yourself. The 5th House's association with confidence does suggest that as we bring these qualities of creative self-actualization forward, we find more within ourselves to feel genuinely good about.

Children are associated with the 5th House. This can sometimes indicate strong karmic bonds with children in one's lifetime, be it one's own or through familial and friendship connections. Being a big kid in one's own right might also be how a North Node here manifests.

In regards to children, one of two scenarios is most possible. The first includes having children early and often. The other involves having children much later in life, if at all. Regardless, the state of one's child-state is often seen as deeply symbolic and spiritually significant.

The North Node in the 5th House comes with a South Node in the 11th House. The 11th House is associated with the connections that we have with friends and groups that we belong to. It can also be related to acquaintances, unions, associations, groups, and fellowships. With the South Node in the 11th house, one might overidentify with their peers and believe that their whole identity is wrapped up in them.

Sometimes, these experiences with our peers will show us the lower end of how friendship can be. It is indirectly and through complicated experiences that we are encouraged to learn the value of trusting ourselves and moving through life more independently.

Perhaps there are situations in early life with friends that lead towards unwise choices. Similarly, it could be that the desire to "go along with the crowd" lends itself to self-defeating actions. The South Node represents the easiest, most default action, or path of least resistance to take. With the North Node in the 5th

House, it is ultimately not so much about being a part of the group. Rather, life opens up when the intuition is trusted. Then genuine joy can be found as well.

North Node in The 6th House

Every spiritual lesson you're meant to learn in this lifetime is part of your role towards moving us all towards greater love and greater wisdom, which I believe is the ultimate purpose of life for us, both individually and collectively. The sign that that North Node is in speaks to the characteristics that you will be encouraged to develop and step into more fully, especially the higher spectrum of that sign over the course of this lifetime. So, when you have your North Node in the 6th House, life is asking you to utilize your day and to use the day to your advantage, not only in terms of how effective you're going to be, but also to consider all the little things you do each day, all the little rituals that you have in place that affirm in some very small moments that you deserve your own love and your own understanding.

In addition, your own growth rate increases exponentially when an understanding that you deserve your own care and attention is affirmed. Ultimately, that is what the 6th House is about. It's about the business of going about your day, doing the things that you need to do, whether it's going to work and being in the work environment or workspace, or going to the same coffee shop that you frequent every day, or the gym, or those little routine exercises you do such as brushing your teeth—all of that is covered by the 6th House. These are little things on the surface, but add up to a big impact over the course of a lifetime. With the North Node here, they add up to a big spiritual impact over the course of the lifetime.

Now, because the 6th House is often connected to the work environment, life will likely present situations where you've got to work with other people, enter the workforce, or be in a work environment of some kind. This is one of the areas of the chart where if your North Node is located here, chances are high that life is going to ask you to step into the work environment. And because this is the part of the sky that has to do co-workers, it is with co-workers that some of the strongest karmic bonds lie. Whether it is instant familiarity with these people, or key life lessons you learn through them, the co-workers, immediate supervisors, clients and customers shape the life path long after they have left your life.

The North Node in the 6th House invites you to look at what kind of spiritual lessons you're learning from your co-workers and what type of relationships you have there, because chances are those people in your life are the ones who are meant to bring you karmic blessings. Now, some of those karmic blessings do come very disguised, depending on how the North Node is aspected (see the next section on aspects). So, if you find yourself having really difficult relationships with the people that you work with, it could be that it is through those difficulties that you come to understand your own spiritual lessons, and through those difficulties, you are able to move towards your own unique version of greater love and wisdom is in your life.

The 6th House speaks to our food-related habits as well. The types of food we prefer and our beliefs around food are found here. The North Node in the 6th House invites a more spiritual approach to eating itself. Whether that involves food choices guided by spiritual or philosophical beliefs, or other reasons that greater awareness around food choices is encouraged, it is through food that you might find a spiritual tool of self- evolution.

A 6th House North Node comes with a South Node in the 12th House. Early life experiences might have asked for isolation. Sometimes these people might have no choice but to spend an extended amount of time on their own, possibly due to illness, or in places like hospitals. At other times, it might be that homeschooling or an unusual or overly protective home led to this sense of being removed from others.

The 12th House is also connected to self-undoing, and the early life might have brought an uncanny tendency towards behaviors that seem to be undermining the self. This might come in the form of early addiction to substances, or other ways in which one's own choices and habits created suffering through undesirable outcomes. The blessing with this placement is that it is these very early experiences that can give way to an acute empathy and a special sense of compassion for others, expressed in small ways everyday.

Perhaps it is through choices made in employment, or through food choices, but it is compassion that is at the heart of what is done in life's smallest moments. And it is in these daily rituals, carried out in sometimes unassuming ways, that great spiritual impact is made.

North Node in The 7th House

The North Node in the 7th House speaks strongly to relationships and one-on-one interactions. The gateway to the 7th House is called the Descendant (DC), and it is exactly opposite the Ascendant (AC). The Ascendant represents what you are projecting. This is also called the rising sign. It represents the immediate first impression you make when you meet somebody and what you are projecting outwards and onto the world. The Descendant represents what you attract back to you based on the Ascendant and that which you are projecting out.

If your North Node is in the 7th house, then chances are people are drawn to you. All of our relationships and connections have a very strong karmic purpose to them, and any relationship or interaction we have holds the promise of moving us in some way towards greater love and greater wisdom, which I believe is the purpose of life. Depending on how that North Node is aspected, or whether any planets that might be near that North Node, will determine the types of people who you tend to attract.

The 7th house speaks to your interactions, especially within your personal relationships or business partnerships, but also to private relationships, such as your marriage or relationship with your significant other. These are the types of relationships that tend to have a contractual agreement associated with them. With The North Node here, these connections can feel especially fated.

I am of the view that if you actually sign a contract with somebody that solidifies a relationship, perhaps a marriage or business partnership, then chances are that this is not the first time you've actually done that with this other Soul over the trajectory of your soul development. Literal contracts we enter into have spiritual significances to them.

A North Node in the 7th House comes hand in hand with a South Node in the 1st House. The early life might have included a need to be especially self-reliant. Perhaps an emphasis was placed on the needs of the self, and some narcissistic tendencies might have presented themselves. Selfishness might have been encouraged. A strong independent streak might have created suffering or discomforting others. And yet, the blessing is to move towards the genuine desire for a more balanced and harmonious way of relating to others as one moves through the world.

The North Node in the 7th House indicates agreements with people where you have to consider another perspective as equal to your own. Whether the connection is personal or professional, the soul lessons will be strong.

North Node in The 8th House

The North Node in the 8th House encourages an understanding of wealth beyond superficial terms. Understanding the self so deeply that you can't help but being reborn. Getting to the root and the essence of yourself, and seeing what really matters. Finding genuine trust in oneself, so that trust issues can be healed, are all part of the journey towards greater love and greater wisdom of this nodal placement.

The 8th house, on a surface level, has to do with shared resources and with money that's not earned through salary, but money that we get from a financial institution, bank or from a lending institution. The kind of money that we might have to apply for and get in one chunk. It also has to do with receiving benefits, paying taxes, and tax refunds. Scholarships, grants, loans, bursaries, and even credit cards are covered in this part of the sky. Inheritances and sharing resources with your spouse are also found here. The North Node here will ask you to interact with financial institutions and understand the deeper dimensions of sharing in practical ways and more.

Life is going to encourage you to move away from focusing on what you own and possess, and instead to find the inner qualities of resilience that are eternal and essential as a more meaningful foundation to your life.

This is where you are asked to check in with yourself, to be honest about how you feel about what you are receiving, whether that is from others, or from the Universe itself. Life will invite you to contemplate how you are provided for by a generous Universe, though not always in the ways you want, but certainly in the ways you need. With this placement, you might find karmic blessings in the form of attracting funding, and the people involved will likely hold many possibilities for karmic blessings in your life.

Beyond the practical indication involving money, this part of the chart also speaks to the psychoanalytic process. Especially beneficial growth and remarkable transformations become possible through engaging therapists. Whether psychological or physical, it is the people who help you to rebuild and to heal that bless your life beyond the obvious and expected ways.

A South Node in the 2nd House can sometimes indicate that the early life might have involved stress or worry around money and possessions. Perhaps there was a sense of there not being enough, or other ways in which you saw a consciousness of poverty, regardless of the practical realities. Perhaps you had to earn money, or felt that you wanted to, as you received the message that money was equal to self-value. The early life might also involve a need to understand and align with money in a healthy way, as over indulgences in purchases become possible. Rooting self-love in more healthy, essential traits beyond the superficial is part of the blessings being cultivated in this lifetime.

The 8th House speaks to trust and resilience. It is the reminder to cultivate an awareness of your ability to trust your own psychological strength, which in turn will allow you to enter into deeper bonds with others. It is true vulnerability that reveals ourselves, mostly to that most unexpected person; the self itself. And it is in this transformative moment of honesty that we know, whatever may happen, you really will be ok.

North Node in The 9th House

The 9th House North Node evolves most when it is allowed to consider new ideas, new people, new languages, and new cultures. Understanding the truths that are relative and personal to each of us, as well as understanding the ideas of the world on a more practical level, are ways in which the soul aligns with its higher purpose of love and wisdom.

One powerful way of accessing the power of the North Node in the 9th house is to travel. Since the Nodes represent what's happening on a level of spirit, it's not necessarily energy that you will be conscious about. Life is likely going to put you in situations where you have to explore or otherwise interact with people who have different backgrounds than yourself. Perhaps different religious ideas, different philosophical ideas about the world, or people who speak different languages. In fact, if you have the North Node in the 9th House, chances are at some point you do have to learn an additional language other than the one you grew up with.

Institutions of higher learning and legal and political institutions are a part of this energy. Pursuing and participating in the idealism of these institutions, by holding them in special esteem and perhaps contributing in key ways to these institutions, are part of what calls you in this lifetime. Karmic contracts and bonds with people within these spaces might be especially strong.

A 9th house North Node brings with it a South Node in the 3rd House. This energy emboldens expression and communication. Early life lessons in sharing and oversharing might present themselves. Perhaps it could have talking too much and saying the wrong thing for the sake of connection with others. Gossip or revealing information that was given in trust can be part of what brings on the early lessons of communication with responsibility.

Strong or complicated connections with early teachers can sometimes be present. Teachers modeling unhealthy beliefs or behaviors that you then have to unlearn might be a part of your path. Additionally, complicated relationships with siblings and cousins might also be present, perhaps through an awareness of how differently you see the world in comparison to them. This tendency might show itself in early life, leaving you to feel separate or distinct in some way.

Words have great power. They can cause joy and also great pain. The misuse of words in the early life might lead you to cultivate higher principles in what you share. An overemphasis on facts, without acknowledging the subtleties of context, might create complex experiences on the way to cultivating a more nuanced way of understanding.

North Node in The 10th House

The cusp of the 10th House is called the Midheaven (MC). This is the astrological zenith in the zodiacal sky. The highest point at the moment of your birth. It represents how we are seen in the broadest sense, usually from faraway or by a large group of people. Public recognition, achievement, career, and fulfillment of life purpose are found here as well. With the North Node in the 10th house, we are asked to consider success and to achieve something meaningful to us. It invites us to cultivate goals and work towards them until they manifest.

The 10th house is the most visible in the sky at the time of birth. With the North Node placed here, you may be asked to be more "visible" than others in some way. This can indicate finding easy opportunities in professions that bring visibility. It may also involve becoming an authority figure within your industry or area of interest, thereby standing out from others in the same field.

However, before you become an authority figure yourself, you will likely have to interact with those with power to help you up the ladder of success. Our bosses and higher ups are found in this same house. The North Node in this area can bring especially powerful karmic bonds with such people, with a sense that the opportunities they grant represents the fulfillment of larger soul contracts. Beyond practical opportunity to rise through the ranks, it is bosses that may make an especially important impression, the kind that shapes your pathway in life long after those relationships are over.

There are times when we have a goal, and even though we are convinced it is something so grand and near impossible, it might actually be a vision much smaller than what the Universe has planed for us. A 10th house North Node invites you to consider that there is a much higher vision for your life that you are meant to align with. The only obstacle would be your own attachment to that other path. Letting go might cause internal struggle and some pain. However, a willingness to consider what a higher contribution could be, outside of what you had planned, can bring a more rewarding path, in practical terms and personally as well.

The North Node in the 10th house brings with it a South Node in the 4th house. The South Node here invites you to move away from sentimentality and a false sense of security that predictability might bring. This is the area that speaks to our comfort zone and the most private part of our lives. You might be learning to "live out loud," and while fear might inform the desire for privacy, life will ask you to live in a way that you wouldn't mind others knowing about.

A 4th house South Node can indicate an especially complex or intense childhood, and perhaps a notably complicated maternal bond. Sometimes, there are behaviors that you demonstrated as a child that you have notable regret or shame around. A South Node placement here says you can't do anything about your past, where you came from, or what happened before you knew better. But you can decide on what you will create and all that you could be. The limits and wounds of the past don't have to characterize your larger contribution. You don't have to continue long established family patterns that don't feel right within your soul.

With a 10th house North Node, success is assured. The soul desires to experience a level of recognition, and on a soul level, the movement towards achievement is constant. Being open to a higher vision to align with helps pave the pathway forwards and upwards.

North Node in The 11th House

The houses that have to do with other people are generally the 3rd, the 7th and the 11th houses. The 3rd house has to do with the people you interact with regularly, especially in your early life, like your siblings and your cousins. It is about who you interact with spontaneously as you go about your day. The 7th House is about the partnerships you form one-on-one, and it is about the commitments you make to other people. The 11th house continues the theme of our connections to others, inviting us to consider our role within organizations, unions, or fellowships that we might belong to, and how these organizations can actually make everyone's life better. When we interact with friends and acquaintances, and anytime we gather with others for personal or professional reasons, it is the 11th house that lights up. The

North Node here makes these spaces, places, and interactions hold that much more personal and spiritual significance for us.

The 11th house is also associated with the collective and with humanity itself. With the North Node here, we are invited think about a lot of people at the same time. A broader perspective on your own actions, reflecting on how they may be impacting humanity and the collective, and thinking about how you can actually do your part to help all of us evolve in a positive direction will be of benefit to you when navigating groups, especially those with humanitarian interests.

Whether it's a union, memberships of different professional organizations, personal support groups, or even spearheading the planning of conferences and events, life is going to ask you to participate and be part of these types of endeavors. Especially strong karmic bonds might be found here, with connections that make a notable emotional or spiritual impression. Informal connections that open more pathways that represent blessings to you. Even attending events where many are gathered together helps you align with the North Node and the promises it holds.

The 11th house has been called a "second childhood," or the house that represents retirement. It is after that we have reached the pinnacle, which the 10th house represents, that we are then able to relax and truly let loose. We are invited to be especially visionary here, wishing and hoping for a better life for ourselves, and for others also. For this reason, this is also the house of hopes and wishes. A North Node here invites an approach that engages a greater sense of play integrated into the life you create. It is also one of the best placements for feeling as if people are on your side to help you achieve the higher wishes and dreams you have for your life.

The 11th house North Node will be accompanied by a South Node in the 5th House. You are moving away from a focus only on your own pleasure, and are invited to elevate your understanding of pleasure. The 5th house is inherently self-focused. It speaks to our focus on the desires of our own hearts. The South Node here can indicate that there was a tendency to be overly ego-driven, insecure, or selfish in the early life. The opportunity involves knowing that as you think about and consider others, your life opens up to more and blessings.

With an 11th House North Node, one is never truly alone. Even with an inherently independent spirit, there are endless opportunities to connect with others. Whether formally or informally, it is the most natural bonds that change us into better versions of ourselves. With the North Node here, they also continue profoundly towards the cultivation of spiritual and practical blessings.

North Node in The 12th House

The 12th house, on the one hand, pertains to meditation and connecting to Source. The North Node in the 12th house is going to ask you to spend time alone and in isolation. Active meditation or entering secluded spaces, like retreats and monasteries, is where you are able to bring forward the karmic blessings promised by the North Node.

Isolation isn't necessarily a practical state. Whenever it is that we are able to step out of our current circumstance and be willing to consider and a more mystical perspective, we are accessing the 12th house. A North Node here will invite us to cultivate this skill, and be better for it.

There are spaces of isolation that may be less than ideal, and where we might not enter willingly. Other spaces of isolation include hospitals or prisons. Places where people have to be or have to stay, that by their very nature separate us from each other. These are the same spaces we enter willingly, through employment or a variety of volunteer efforts. A North Node in the 12th house might require you to go into these different types of institutions. Regardless of how we get there, the promise of spiritual and practical blessings can be found here.

The 12th house has a link with addiction. Addiction can indicate a soul desire to experience emotional and spiritual bliss. Within the sense of being completely plugged into Source, creation energy is often described this way; blissful. Thus, if your North Node is in your 12th house, then you're being asked to manifest this energy and its highest possible sense, and in the healthiest way possible. A part of understanding the pathway forward might sometimes involves drug abuse in the earlier part of life, as part of learning about the spiritual energy within. True blessings emerge when substances are not needed to appreciate the connection to Source that has always been there.

A North Node in the 12th house will accompany a South Node is in the 6th House. The 6th House invites being present in your body, and has to do with what you do as you go about your day. Things that you need to do as far as going to work, going to the gym and taking care of your physical body are all found in this house. A South Node in the 6th house reminds you not to get lost in the mundane areas of life. The material world is ultimately illusionary. It is a valuable tool to help us integrate spiritual lessons. The blessing with this placement is the cultivation of the deeper meaning brings ease as you move through the world.

We may look to the 12th house as an especially mystical, imaginative, and compassionate area of life. A North Node here can bring rewards through the development of the imagination, especially in artistic forms, including music and poetry. The growth of a more mystical appreciation grows throughout the lifetime, and one of the blessings indicated here can be as a teacher of deep, spiritual truths to others. Compassion and empathy are thought to be hallmarks throughout religious traditions. Again and again, we have received the message that to have genuine care for others brings us especially closer to a higher power. A North Node in the 12th house will invite opportunities to be blessed through the experience of selfless giving and sharing. We are all connected to everyone and everything. The affirmation of this great truth is the greatest source of compassion there is.

Planets in Aspect to the Nodes

Aspects and Transits

Every astrological symbol, from the sign, planet, asteroid, chart point, or house in an astrology chart has a spectrum of expression. Some expressions can be enlightened and classified as more "positive." Other expressions can be more mundane, immediate, or can reflect the shadow side of that sign or house.

The North Node is a calculated chart point, and it is a powerful and important point in prediction because it speaks of how the Universe is leading us to greater love and greater wisdom. It also represents a point of karmic agreements and karmic contracts.

The North Node will show us the path we will take and the people we will meet to truly discover our potential and what we should do in this life; and because this will happen on a spiritual level, we will have situations in life in which we will bring forward characteristics covered by the sign of the North Node.

The planets in aspect to the North Node will bring enlightened, esoteric, and emotionally focused qualities. Those with planets in conjunction with the North Node tend to attract people who somehow evoke what that planet is like as an archetype, playing roles as suggested by the planet's mythological, archetypal role. These people will constantly encourage the soul represented in the chart to remember its destiny, to become more of what the soul most desired to be when it incarnated. For example, Jupiter conjunct the North Node can bring teachers and professors that fill this role. Venus on the North Node will be lovers who fulfill this function. We will dive into each planet in aspect to each of the Nodes in more detail in a moment.

The North Node speaks to just how it is that we go about evolving, pulling ourselves into the future, healing the past, and actually fulfilling those promises that we made to ourselves. The North Node represents a doorway, and when there is a transiting planet that aspects the North Node, that doorway opens. New people, opportunities, and ideas can enter when a planet is about to move over the North Node. It represents a pull into the future. When a planet aspects the North Node, particularly by conjunction, often a new person enters who represents the archetype of that planet. In addition, when the North Node is aspected, it could be opportunities that ask us to develop the sign qualities, or develop ourselves in that area of life that that house represents, which is to say that we are the present ourselves. Planets aspecting the North Node will accelerate and bring in people who are an intimate part of the process.

Of course, we can help the process by making the most of fortunate transits to the Nodes. By being active, we cast the net wide, from which karmic blessings may find us. For example, if you know you've got your North Node in the 6th House, and I see a conjunction coming up of Jupiter, I would suggest being busy at work, start going to the gym, and start learning more about health and other 6th House matters. *All of these are going to help you gather the experiences that you need, in order for you to meet the people that you need, for you to have the experiences that are going to help you to pull into the future, which is going to help you move towards your evolution and fulfill those promises you made to yourself.

Where the North Node is found in the chart, we tend to manifest the higher expression of that sign and also the most esoteric and enlightened understandings of that house. The planets in aspect to the Nodes operate along with this principle as well.

The Nodes operate as a gateway from which people enter from the North Node, and leave from the South Node. The appreciation of people as karmic contracts becomes heightened when there is a planet in aspect to one of the Nodes.

The South Node represents the most immediate past life from which we are moving away, something we need to heal in this life or that we really want to get to the opposite end of. With the South Node, we may find ourselves drawn towards behaviors that reflect the shadow, or lower vibration of that sign. This tendency tends to be strongest before the first Saturn Return at about the age of twenty-nine. After this time, once life and astrology have ushered in adulthood, there is a natural strengthening and move towards the North Node, especially if the soul is conscious of its evolution.

Planets in aspect to the South Node tend to manifest themselves as people who bring forward the lower, more immediate and more literal qualities of that sign. We may attract people playing the roles that these planets represent, who we may feel an immediate connection to. We may find ourselves feeling as if we have known people in a previous lifetime. Because it is the South Node, these people might be externalized versions of the lower qualities of that planet.

I have found that it really helps to anthropomorphize the planets as the ancients did. They thought of them as physical embodiments of gods or goddesses. It may be useful for us to learn a little about mythology, as it can help us create a stronger, personal connection with the planets (See more about the myth and cultivating a personal connection with the astrological planets in my book, *Prayers To The Sky*). It is precisely the personal connection we make to the sky that will determine how that sky speaks to us. You cannot have astrology without the astrologer; astrology needs us as much as it needs the astrologer to interpret the sky and bring meaning to it.

Astrology is an act of poetry. It takes the visual symbols of the sky and translates them into words. I would invite you to consider the relationships with these energies as you move towards interpreting aspects of planets to the Nodes. The planets each have their own needs, their own expression and drives. They have certain characteristics and roles they play that might show up in the people we attract. In short, when you cultivate this relationship with the sky and make astrology a spiritual practice, you will strengthen your practice and become a better astrologer.

Any aspects made to one of the Nodes will also involve the other. For example, a planet that creates a square to one Node is actually in a T-square with both, as it stands at a midpoint between the North and South Nodes. A trine to one Node will accompany a sextile to the other. And conjunctions to one Node, will oppose the other. In this way, you can't have a planet aspecting only one. The planet is intimately involved in the journey towards the future, as indicated by the North Node, and in healing the past, as indicated by the South Node.

Determining Strength Of An Aspect

Not all aspects are created equal. The nature of the transit will determine how strong it is.

Conjunction: This is the strongest type of aspect. This is when a planet joins one of the Nodes within the chart. In the case of the North Node, a conjunction brings someone new, exemplified as the archetype of that planet. This person will represent karmic blessings. Because a conjunction of the North Node does, by its very definition, opposes the South Node, this beginning carries a movement away from the past. Conversely, conjunctions of planets to the South Node bring with them closures, sometimes dramatic, where people and situations represented by that planet exit the life. With this closure, comes an understanding that this end is allowing the chance to move forward and begin again. These closures are often accompanied by gratitude, though not always immediately.

Harmonious Aspects: these consist of Trines and Sextiles. One will always accompany the other where it comes to aspecting the Nodes. Both are considered easy, or favorable, aspects. The stronger aspect of the 2 is the trine. If the trine is being made to the North Node, karmic blessings may follow, though they might be subtle at times. Emphasis is placed on the personal qualities being developed in alignment with the North Node's sign qualities. These qualities help move you towards characteristics that feel like they create more opportunities in your life.

When the Trine is to the South Node, you realize that the blessing is in the qualities, as represented by its sign, that you are leaving behind. You understand your past behaviors differently, and are motivated to move forward and do better, by integrating more qualities of the North Node.

Hard Aspects: This is the T-square, when a planet squares the North and South Nodes simultaneously, and is considered a hard aspect. As mentioned earlier, a planetary square to one of the Nodes necessarily will square the other, thereby setting increased tension between the two. A T-Square of the Nodes represents how that planetary energy holds power, through tension, to help you understanding your soul path. It can feel as if the needs of that planet are at odds with what the soul desires, and yet, it is this very tension that spurs exploration and action, that ultimately aids in the evolution of the soul in this lifetime.

Natal Planets Conjunct the Nodes

Natal planets in aspect with the Nodes have a heightened potency. They speak to an archetypal energy that is either being healed in this life, as through the South Node, or that will help us move into our future of honoring and fulfilling the deeper lessons of the soul, as is the case of the North Node.

Regardless of the type of aspect, we can consider them as part of our karmic blessings. The activation of the Nodes by a birth planet will always bring us in contact with people who will help us along our path towards greater love and greater wisdom in this life, fulfilling those promises we made to ourselves and fulfilling the purpose of our incarnation.

Depending on the nature of the planet, you either are going to be invited to embrace it and see right away how great this is, or you're going to fight it. There's no use fighting it because this is all happening on a level of karma, especially when something has served its purpose and it needs to go. It's a good thing that it needs to go because that, in turn, will make the North Node that much stronger, the North Node that desires to pull you into the future.

When a planet aspects the Nodes within the Natal chart, the energy is with you always. You will likely continually feel that the themes we will discuss for that placement show up again and again, throughout the lifetime.

Transiting Planets in Aspect to the Nodes

When transiting planets aspect the Nodes, it represents a powerful energy visiting for a time. The interpretation is the same, but the application is over a determined period, rather than the lifetime. However, the effects can be felt long after, as any aspects to the Nodes can shift your direction in remarkable ways, sometimes, for a lifetime.

The Nodes are of prime importance when it comes to prediction, especially when it comes to planets conjunct the Nodes, because when they conjunct the South Node, it indicates some larger lessons, karmic endings, doors closing, or an understanding of what has served its karmic purpose in your life. But when planets conjunct the North Node, it is as if a doorway opens from which new people, new opportunities, and new understandings have a way of entering, bringing with them karmic blessings into our lives.

Regardless of whether it's the South Node or the North Node being aspected by a planet, this energy is part of aligning you powerfully with the direction in which the soul desires to go. Aspects help in honoring the purpose of the incarnation, and to align us with that higher vision of ourselves for this lifetime.

Sun in Aspect to the Nodes

The Sun is Regal. The King or Queen Principle in the astrology chart. It is where we find our center. Where we know we deserve to shine and be seen. It is where we stand in our own royalty. The Sun isn't as much as who we are, but whom it is we desire to fully become in this lifetime, as our most celebrated and enlightened selves.

To be born with the Sun in conjunction with one of the Nodes indicates to be born in a period between or during eclipses. This alone suggests a powerful lifetime, where there is an awareness that you are packing in the lessons of several lifetimes into one. This life can feel especially filled with strong, fated moments that dramatically align you with opportunities in new and unexpected ways. It also indicates a powerful will and life force. Depending on how you use it, notable personal power can be for the good of yourself or others.

A conjunction of the Sun to the South Node can denote special challenges. The Sun is who we are consciously becoming, while the South Node is what the soul desires to move away from. As the lower vibrations of the sign placement of the South Node are already heightened, they are more likely to show up as dominant characteristics with the Sun here.

Where we are projecting this energy onto others, we might attract especially attention seeking people, who we feel have a light that we might find desirable to model, as we ourselves find familiarity with this light. At the same time, we might see how these relationships have unhealthy characteristics that need to be healed. As to its association to Royalty, those born with Sun conjunct the South Node might have a knack for attracting "Drama Queens" into their lives, especially in the area of life indicated by the house.

The Sun in conjunction with the North Node brings a soul with a strong sense of its own destiny. The soul understands, on a deep level, that it is meant to step into the light, to shine, to be seen. By becoming fully one's self, it simultaneously honors the purpose of the incarnation at the same time. On a soul level, this person knows what it's here to do.

The Sun conjunct North Node types will attract people who are metaphorical kings, or king-makers. People who are able to acknowledge the destiny of a person and bring it forward. They may be people who are theatrical in some way, whether by profession or in characteristics. Actors, particularly vivid teachers, those who have cultivated a role that is respected in their career, and leaders in many industries are the types of people that are drawn towards the person with Sun conjunct their North Node. This is an especially fortunate placement, that indicates success in the things you like about yourself, and a high level of charisma.

Aspects between the Sun and the Nodes can represent a soul that has come into this life with a strong connection to its past lives. They will find themselves very early in life, understanding some essentials about their identity. When it is a harmonious connection, the full embrace of their soul's past, and integrating it into the future they are becoming, can be seamless.

However, when it is a hard aspect, there might be internal or external resistance to the path of the soul. On an external level, the early childhood environment might not feel like a supportive space where one can truly be themselves. More personally, if the person is to align more fully with the higher, more loving vision for this lifetime, some part of the ego must be surrendered. Once this occurs, and spiritual alignment is prioritized, the qualities that come forward bring special reward.

Transiting Sun in Aspect to the Nodes

The Sun goes through a different sign every month, so it will conjunct the South Node once a year and it will conjunct the North Node once a year as well. Similarly, the trine and sextile each will happen twice a year to each of the Nodes. The t-square happens twice a year, at the exact midpoints of the zodiacal sky.

The Sun, as a regal principle, invites clarity into where and how we are ultimately meant to shine, and where we can tap into our sense of worthiness. It is where and how we, in our own way, desire to be King or Queen.

The Sun conjunct the South Node brings clarity on what should no longer be part of life, and it lightens our burden. It tends to be a time when we are reminded to let go of people, places, things and situations that no longer serve the soul's path. We are made lighter and freer. People might exit our lives, sometimes rather dramatically. It does make for a good story!

There is often a sense that the closures taking place are right, that the time for this ending has come, and that brings a sense of relief. This conjunction brings an understanding of the things holding us back. We are invited to bring closure so these behaviors, environments, or people no longer hold us back anymore. At the same time, there is excitement about who you might become in this lifetime, as you move forward from here.

When the Sun moves over the North Node, it brings personal clarity. New people can enter now who, in some way, can be very confident and bold, who will boost our confidence as well. It is a time when we can attract people who affirm a healthy sense of self- confidence within us. It can also be a powerful time to shine, to take a chance on what we truly want, or to hope to impress those who might help light a pathway forward for us.

However, as much as we might work with the Nodes consciously, some of the more meaningful occurrences at this time will be by chance, or by fate. We meet someone who gives us advice or insights which, in a surprising way, end up changing our direction. We attract new experiences that show us whom it is we could be, if we trusted our soul desires.

This placement reminds me of the Sun as Apollo. Apollo was the Greek God of rationality, but also of prophecy. Either one of these can play out with the Sun over the North Node. We may have a situation where we receive some type of prophecy, that will help us understand our direction, and we may find a deeper sense of fulfillment. It can also be a time of a well thought out, rational decision that shapes our destiny for a long time to come.

When we experience a harmonious transit of the Sun to the Nodes, we might have an experience that helps us recognize the things within us that we can feel good about. Easy opportunity finds us, that feels natural and right. When it is a hard transit, we might have the feeling that what our soul wants, and what the ego self wants, are 2 different things. It can be a time of some lesson that is hard won, but ultimately shapes our pathway forward.

The Sun is warm, and when it transits the Nodes, it is a time when we are stepping into an awareness of where our personal evolution might be heading. This period of time helps us bring forward things that we like in ourselves.

Moon in Aspect to the Nodes

The Moon is the quintessential maternal figure. This can be considered in its externalized sense, as in our relationship with our mother and other older women in our lives, especially in childhood. But there is the internalized mother archetype as well. How well are we able to care and nurture for ourselves and how we feel about it speaks to this internalized mother archetype. The Moon brings this energy into other situations, to consider where and how is it that we are a mother to others. Is it only to our children, or is it in other types of relationships as well?

When the Moon is in aspect to the Nodes in the natal chart, it will bring with it repeated lessons in motherhood. This lesson can show up in all kinds of relationships, including the one we have with ourselves. Similarly, attracting karmic archetypes of people who nourish us, in a variety of ways, will likely be part of the life path.

The Moon represents food, as it is one of the more immediate and mundane ways in which we nourish ourselves. When you have the Moon in conjunction with the South Node, the early life might have been characterized by food for emotional comfort without connecting to what might nourish you more deeply. There might be an unhealthy relationship with food that needs to be healed, and through healing, we find transcendence and spiritual growth as we grow older.

In some instances, this can also suggest a need of literal nourishment and extended care as a child. As such, notable caregivers in early life, like someone who attends to their needs, will be part of the expression of this placement. Some of those bonds may require 'unlearning' some unhealthy forms of self-care in later life.

The Moon in conjunction to the South Node could indicate a person in early life, who is demanding of or feels like a drain on personal energy. Care is needed not to recreate that experience as one gets older. The first major platonic or romantic relationships might involve attracting people in need of our care, rather than those who are interested in the healthy sharing that relationships usually ask. We might find relationships that feel emotionally draining, or perhaps draining in other ways, like with our time or our money. Ultimately, the purpose of the incarnation is to honor the North Node, so through trial and error, we can come to understand how to have a healthy relationship with one's own mother, and within our relationships as well.

The Moon in conjunction with the North Node indicates a soul who is on a journey towards understanding emotional fulfillment and spiritual nourishment. Their soul has a desire to be at ease and comfortable with who they are. It is through the intuitive, emotional channels that a sense of purpose is found. They may find themselves attracting mother figures. These are people who genuinely care about them, with whom they feel a mother-child connection. These people awaken our own maternal instincts, regardless of what the gender identity may be. They teach and model healthy forms of self-care, that change our direction in a multitude of positive ways.

When the Moon is in conjunction with the North Node, strong female figures, reminiscent of the mother archetype, occupy a prominent place in our success, evolution, and life path. The lessons we learn through them help align us with greater karmic blessings well after those connections dissolve.

The Moon in hard, square aspect to the Nodes in the natal chart can indicate the mother archetype feeling like a heavy karmic burden, especially in early life. This could indicate a heightened sense of obligation to the mother that arose from challenging early circumstances. Sometimes the perception is that the challenges were 'shared' by the two, so they were 'in it together'. While this expression does offer opportunities for growth and evolution of the relationship, a strong sense of lifelong responsibility might always remain. However, if the Moon is in harmonious aspect with the Nodes in the natal chart, there will likely be a sense that the early maternal figures, like our mother, worked to bring forward the child's sense of safety and affirmed a personal sense of destiny.

Transiting Moon in Aspect to the Nodes

The Moon will conjunct the South and North Nodes every twenty-eight and a half days. As the fastest main celestial body we use in astrology, it takes the Moon that long to zip around the zodiac. Therefore, we get to experience the Moon conjunct the Nodes many times over, especially during the course of a full lifetime. Twice within that twenty-eight and a half day cycle, the Moon will sextile and trine each of the Nodes twice. The T-square to the Nodes will occur twice in that lunar cycle as well.

The more often we experience a celestial energy, the less impactful it is. For example, we might experience an outer planet conjunction with one of the Nodes just once, over the course of a lifetime. This rare transit to a natal chart undoubtedly brings big changes; everything can shift during times such as these. When these types of rare conjunctions happen, the best approach is to go with this flow and surrender to where the journey of an extended transit like this wants to take you. Circumstances can change drastically, as we adjust to what wants to leave and the new opportunities coming in.

When the transiting Moon is making a conjunction to one of the natal Nodes, it is a subtle energy, and usually personal. An understanding on your part about what needs to happen. A personal point of clarity as to what you really feel. A decision that feels right in your soul. It can be notable, but we often have more agency.

When the Moon conjuncts the South Node once every 4 weeks, you will likely understand what has served its purpose in your life, for now. This can indicate an internal shift, brought about through an emotional understanding. Sometimes, the Moon on the South Node will bring forgiveness. The things that really annoyed you a few days or weeks ago will be clear and you will let them go. The Moon has to do with home, so if you've had some practical or familial issues in your home, this is the time you'll understand how to solve them, leave them in the past and be done with it.

Be mindful that the South Node is a place that can drain you of energy, and when the Moon conjuncts the South Node, you may attract situations that make you aware of where you feel like you are giving too much. This aspect asks us to be more mindful of our emotional energy and step up our self-care. This can be a great day to decide you will avoid situations and people you know can be stressful, if possible.

The Moon conjunct the North Node can bring women into our lives who are motherly and caregiving. We can get good advice from women at this time that will help clarify our direction, These might be established bonds or random interactions with

130

strangers. They still have a quality of good advice lending itself to emotional calm.

Transiting Moon in harmonious aspect to the Nodes will help us understand the direction that feels emotionally fulfilling, and what resonates with the soul and spirit. It can be as simple as stumbling upon a good meal, or feeling especially cozy at home. It will be an internal understanding that will bring clarity. It can point the way to what you need to feel a greater sense of emotional balance and ease. The transiting T-square can indicate a moment of tension, which helps you make a choice that feels right to you. It might also be a time when you see the value in 'the path of least resistance' and practice emotional acceptance.

Mercury in Aspect to the Nodes

Mercury has been conceptualized as the Messenger of The Gods, often depicted with wings on his feet, moving mighty fast. Mercury zips around the zodiac, spending about 3-4 weeks a year per sign, in normal circumstances. However, Mercury is rarely whatever could be called 'normal'. That would be boring. In many mythologies, he is described as a trickster figure. Constantly fluid and flowing, in mind and body. Free to be as androgynous as he was limitless. Beloved and free to love. He's also free to go back over old ground and change his mind, and he grants us the same, every time Mercury goes into one of his famous retrograde phases 3-4 times a year.

His ability to be peers with everyone, regardless of status or station, lends to his association with siblings and cousins. They are our very first peers. And like the siblings we grow with, we often share personal languages and develop with them. Mercury in conjunction with the South Node can bring complicated and deep bonds with these very types of people. This can sometimes give way to feelings of being easily provoked by our siblings and cousins, well into adulthood, in a way that brings forward parts of ourselves we don't always like.

Solace can sometimes be found in school friends, with whom there might be deep bonds. Perhaps one was mistaken for a twin to you. However, the South Node can also indicate extremes, and being too immersed in the early schooling environment might have led to intense relationships with your fellow classmates.

The mind, its practical and metaphorical functions, are the providence of Mercury. Mercury placed on the South Node can indicate a speech or learning impediment, which takes special effort to heal from. The axiom 'words can cut like a knife' might be a notable lesson that either comes about through not enough caution, or lends to over caution, with words in early life.

In its highest manifestation, the mind can have a different, more nostalgic way of thinking. In the right environment, filled with stories of myth and history, you might have found this faculty encouraged. Channeled well, Mercury here can help you give voice to your previous lives, helping you to feel their presence on your consciousness.

Mercury in conjunction with the North Node will bring people to your life that carry Mercurial qualities. You might have a knack for attracting especially talkative or brilliant types. These are people who help you cultivate opportunities in all kinds of ways, but most will be centered in expression. Some will help you express yourself, cultivate a sense of spontaneously, and to find your voice. They might encourage a more enlightened sense of how you see the world.

These mercurial qualities might also be superficial; special bonds with those who don't embrace strict or limited gender roles, and are therefore free to be their own unique selves. There might also be classmates and other peers, with whom we feel free to be truly ourselves. Our bonds with our siblings, cousins and neighbors might be especially blessed, with genuine companionship and practical blessings.

When Mercury is in harmonious aspect to the Nodes in the natal chart, we feel ever encouraged in early life, by those we consider our equals. There are natural connections and re-connections with those who were our peers in childhood. There might be rewards throughout the lifetime, which come from our ability to express ourselves in words; whether written or spoken.

In hard aspect, hard work is put in to communicate the way you'd like to express yourself. This may first show up in needing extra time to understand your school studies, and evolve into needing time to work through your own thoughts before you decide what to share. This might also indicate an unusual way of speech or thought processes, that make you unusual to some, but help you find your own, if limited, peer group, with whom you find genuine camaraderie.

Transiting Mercury in Aspect to the Nodes

Mercury will make either 1 conjunction per year to one of the Nodes, or 3. It all depends on whether that conjunction happens during one of the infamous retrograde phases. Similarly, the harmonious aspects can happen either 4 times a year, with 2 sextiles and 2 trines each, or up to 12 of these aspects in a calendar year. The T-square can occur between 2 and up to a possible 6 times within a calendar year.

Mercury represents messages and communications. It speaks to receiving news and holding key talks. Notable social media engagement can express itself during aspects of Mercury to the Nodes.

Mercury conjunctions to the South Node can indicate an important ending or turning point, defined by a closure. A neighbor might leave the area. An important change in the relationship with a sibling or cousin might occur. As Mercury is often retrograde, it will sometimes make three aspects to the South Node, and this will represent an ongoing conversation. It doesn't always mean that a person actually leaves, but it could mean that a pattern or way of being within a certain relationship with a sibling, a cousin, a neighbor, or a peer is transforming.

Transiting Mercury conjunct the South Node might also bring knowledge of what needs to end, in order to strengthen yourself and your path. It is information that makes a difference, helping to refine the pathway of a given endeavor. however, with the South Node, it is closings that come from this information. Awareness can occur through conversations or other communications. We might receive a literal message, that allows us to see things differently.

Transiting Mercury conjunct the North Node invites you to pay attention to messages. This is the literal symbol of a message delivered, that changes your direction in a favorable direction. It might be as subtle as getting an insight or seeing a social media post online, receiving a text or even a phone call. The overall characteristic is of something new coming in, that represents a blessing. This transit can move you forward on a soul level, or forward in more practical ways.

Transiting conjunctions to the North Node can bring new connections that feel light, easy, and freeing. These are people who might help you communicate better, or are simply easy to talk to. The types of people that might come in at this time would carry karmic blessings or, at the very least, would carry some sort of message that we need to understand where the Universe is prompting us to go.

Mercury in harmonious aspect to the Nodes will make it that much easier to speak up and speak out, and to communicate in ways that help us feel good about ourselves. This is a friendly time, and wonderful for getting together with people you consider your contemporaries. Those with whom you can talk to about anything. It is also helpful in situations where it could be advantageous to communicate naturally and effectively. For example, interviews and meetings can feel effectual at this time. Hard aspects to the Nodes can have us feeling like we said the wrong thing at the wrong time, so it's wise to be especially mindful with what we say during this transit. And yet, it is through communication itself that we are refined and learn how to express ourselves as we most intend.

Venus in Aspect to the Nodes

Venus is the Love Goddess, and she is fun. Her association with social graces and lush events, along with the pleasures of being alive, make her a favorite when aspected within the natal chart. But like all things, too much of a good thing can loose some of its appeal.

Venus in conjunction with the South Node represents people who have a strong past life romantic karma that they are working out in this life. These types of people tend to make romantic decisions in the early part of life that they may regret after their Saturn Return, once they turn 30. There tends to be a strong understanding of who they are linked to. They also have strong reactions towards their romantic partners in the first stage of the connection, when they meet, and they seem to know immediately if this is the person who they want to be with. A strong familiarity is a theme with their first romantic partners.

Furthermore, Venus conjunct the South Node in the natal chart can mean that these people will find their soul-mates very early in life. However, it is also possible that there life is defined by more than one person they see as a soul mate. Just as Venus had many loves, these people too may find this to be the case. Early life might be characterized as being 'clingy' with partners, until they learn to advance this energy forward, placing emphasis on the North Node opposition that this placement inherently contains. From there, people are able to act as compliments as they align with a higher vision for their life.

Romantic connections in early life could be completely different from romantic connections in later stages. They might have drastically different romantic inclinations in the first part of life than in later stages. These inclinations might be superficial; their preference in the appearance of possible partners might alter dramatically as they grow. They might also be more personal, seeking dramatically different power and relational dynamics from one stage of life to the next.

Venus has been understood differently, and as the ruler of Taurus and Libra, it is also expressed differently. *The Symposium* by Plato described the differences between Earthly Aphrodite and Heavenly Aphrodite. We as astrologers can draw correlations to the Earthly expression of Venus as most associated with her

Taurus rulership. Similarly, her Heavenly association can be attributed to her rulership of Libra.

Aphrodite has been depicted as enjoying Earthly pleasures; enjoying the five senses through food and wine, and enjoying the physical experience of connection with another person. Venus in conjunction with the South Node is more likely to manifest as an Earthly Aphrodite. We can consider those who demonstrate an inclination towards design, fashion, make up, and other aesthetic ways of enjoying Venusian energy as associated with this placement.

However, Venus in conjunction with the North Node will bring a more Heavenly understanding of Venus. Discovering what beauty of thoughts will consist of uniquely for you will be part of the life path. Finding beauty in ideas, forms, and truth are also considered heavenly pursuits. Venus conjunct the North Node invites us to align the energy of love with a higher calling, higher vision, or perhaps a Higher Power.

Venus in conjunction with the North Node is a natal aspect of blessing. Venus represents being worthy of receiving, so her placement here will help attract people who are generous, as part of affirming that lesson. Venus in conjunction with the North Node would bring people into life carrying karmic blessings, people who are likely female or who have strong female energy. Who are and who look beautiful. These connections are not exclusively romantic. Blessing related to prosperity are likely, especially in

Venusian related industries like art, design, beauty, joyous events, and the cultivation of grace.

Venus in harmonious aspect to the Nodes encourages trust in what is inherently fun or easy to do. Talents carried forward from other lives find opportunities to be developed, which in turn leads to practical opportunities for financial gain. Hard aspects from Venus to the Nodes in the natal chart can suggest a tendency towards, or fear of, overindulgence. It might be seen as a hinderance to what the soul desires to do. There might be resistance in depending on others, or allowing others to be too involved in the cultivation of blessings, for fear of complicating bonds. For all this, the motivation is there to create something beautiful to you, which holds personal and spiritual satisfaction.

Transiting Venus in Aspect to the Nodes

Venus will normally spend about a year moving though the zodiac, and will retrograde about every year and a half. Her retrograde will take place over the period of about 6 weeks. Over the course of a year, Venus will usually make 2 trines and 2 sextiles to each of the Nodes, and 2 T-squares to the Nodes. She will conjunct each of the Nodes once. During her rare retrograde phase, these aspects might be multiplied up to 3 times each.

Transiting Venus conjunct the natal South Node would signify the end of a situation, and there might be a sense of this being a favorable ending. Venus, known as a 'lower benefic' in traditional astrology, affirms that this transit might be seen as a blessing.

The ending is usually realized quickly. A romantic relationship could end, but this also suggests a turning point within an established bond. A depth of understanding that ultimately brings a defining understanding.

Transiting Venus conjunct the natal South Node can speak to the end of a pattern within a relationship. The end of understanding where someone fits in to a personal, spiritual lesson, and where they don't. It also could be the end of a certain expectation within a relationship, which ultimately brings more happiness.

Venus conjunct the natal South Node by transit can also suggest the end of a financial situation, a financial shift, or change of income, but this is not the case most often. More likely where overindulgence has been the case, this transit allows us to acknowledge it, and change our ways.

Transiting Venus conjunct the natal North Node suggests a new person or new opportunity. This could bring with it some kind of romantic experience that ends up changing our understanding of what love will mean going forward from here, what role it will have in life, or what a more enlightened type of love could be. A larger spiritual lesson may present itself through a romantic interaction. What a healthier, more evolved love is going to look like for you in the future starts to become more clear.

This placement can bring a new understanding, or the feeling of a new chapter, if you are in an established bond. This transit can sometimes bring financial opportunity. A new social opportunity, to have fun and socialize, can be part of this transit as well.

When Venus is in harmonious aspect to the nodes, it denotes easy connections with others and lovely, gracious exchanges. This can be a wonderful time to shop for clothing, makeup, or visit the hairdresser, as the results are more likely to be favorable. A square to the Nodes can denote a sense of dissatisfaction where is comes to matters related to love, beauty or money. These are not the best days to cultivate a Venusian connection, so if you can help it, avoid trying new things where it comes to your look. The dissatisfaction might be inviting you to look deeper, and find a sense of self acceptance at this time. You are perfect just as you are!

Mars in Aspect to the Nodes

Mars is the God of War and also the God of Athletics. According to ancient prayers, Mars also pertains to emotional control and strategic, effective action. Mars also invites us to connect to a sense of integrity, exerting yourself in the world from a place of self-knowledge. When we summon our spiritual warrior, taking risks towards our enlightenment, we are connecting with the best that Mars can be.

The energy of Mars encourages us to learn how to take advantage of our own sacred, warrior energy. Natal mars conjunct the South Node might represent a person who enters this life with strong physical energy. Early opportunities in athletics is possible, sometimes accompanied with the recognition of athletic or physical talent.

However, the immediate application of natal Mars conjunct the South Node, can be that you attract people who will awaken this sacred warrior within by evoking feelings of 'fight or flight'. A less enlightened form of a warrior's spiritual energy can come forward in these scenarios. A sense that the early environment was a metaphorical battlefield, or a confrontational environment, might be there.

There might also be a sense of coming into this life with some anger issues to heal. There might have been an especially complicated early environment, with emotional extremes or a sense of intensity. In rare cases, there might have been indirect or direct violence. Strong male figures were likely associated with defining experiences, possibly characterized by their high energy or feelings of disorder that accompanied them.

Mars in conjunction with the North Node in the natal chart operates on the very opposite of the spectrum. The tendency is to attract people who will inspire your spiritual and sacred warrior energy in healthy ways. Experiences that invite you to consider what higher qualities are worth fighting for can present themselves. A spiritual perspective on free-will helps in understanding power, so that you can be yourself in the world with absolute self-knowledge and absolute confidence.

Personal life force grows with age, and unlike others, people with natal Mars conjunct their North Node might become especially energetic with age. People who work within fields of the military, the police, athletics, and those carrying strong, masculine characteristics hold special potential to open doors of opportunity in all kinds of ways.

Mars is an independent energy, that will allow you to attract many experiences. The potential to summon an entrepreneurial spirit, rooted in a singular truth in the soul, holds special promise for reward.

Harmonious aspects from Mars to the Nodes in the natal chart suggest easy energy and a child like enthusiasm benefit your pathway towards easy opportunities. The cultivation of physical strength and personal will aids you in connecting with those who might help your practical and spiritual growth. Hard aspects between Mars and the Nodes in the natal chart come with notable motivation, and sometimes endless energy, that might not be easy for others to understand. An attitude of 'I'll show you!" Brings the motivation needed to see through obstacles, and secure success.

Transiting Mars in Aspect to the Nodes

Mars takes about 2 years to go around the zodiac, spending some 7 weeks per sign in that period of time. However, the retrograde phase will take place every 18 months or so, and will last about 2 months. Conjunctions to each of the Nodes will happen once during that time frame, for each of the 2 Nodes. Harmonious aspects of the trine and sextile will take place once a year. The hard T-square also happens once a year. If these transits occur with Mars in a larger retrograde cycle, these aspects can multiply up to 3 times each.

Transiting Mars conjunct the natal South Node attracts experiences that help us connect with personal power. In most cases, this power is good, but in some cases this can represent a time that feels emotionally or physically challenging. High energy and high adrenaline moments can denote feeling drained of life force. A good rule is to be especially cautious of your environment and of accidents at the height of this transit. For some, Mars conjunctions to the natal South Node help us understand obstructions to healthy expressions of power.

Another notable point is, the very nature of this energy is physical, and physical energy isn't only worked out in the gym. Attracting experiences to be physically intimate with another may suddenly show up at this time, and strong, immediate attractions can be felt physically. This transit does not, in itself, denote a relationship. It can denote flirtation that moves to passion.

Like any conjunction to the South Node, an applicable interpretation is people leaving. These might be people who have annoyed you in the past, or there may be a feeling of having had enough their presence in your life. Some of these exits might be dramatic or passionate in fashion. Sometimes, it might feel like a notable loss. Mars is considered the lower malefic, and there are situations where the loss feels undesirably sudden, or evokes an unintended strong reaction. Regardless, endings that happen with planets conjunct the South Node have a depth of understanding. The person, place, thing, or situation has served its karmic purpose. This end aligns you with greater love and greater wisdom, whether it is evident immediately or not.

If you are approaching the chart with greater consciousness, this time can bring with it an understanding of how to use your free will intelligently. Having enough understanding of yourself and your own agency can help you make the most of this time. Using previous transits of Mars conjunct the natal South Node well shows up in self-knowledge gained. Enough to know where your energy is being wasted, and realizing that you don't want to put any energy in draining situations anymore.

Transiting Mars conjunct the natal North Node is a powerful transit. It tends to bring in a figure, usually with strong masculine traits, who has a strong presence, or has a strong will. It also attracts people into your life who encourage you to bring those qualities forward from within yourself. Mars is a sacred and spiritual warrior, or simply a warrior, soldier or athlete. These archetypes will be inspired in you at this time, so you may find that you attract athletes into your life at this time. You may attract someone who practices some sort of martial arts or spiritual arts, or decide to learn these practices for yourself.

The Universe is going to encourage you to tap into your sacred warrior energy. Channeling this energy wisely can help bring

148

forward the higher qualities of this transit of Mars to the natal North Node. Something as simple as going to the gym is a healthy way to tap and release this energy. Alternatively, life might present you with opportunities to harness your warrior energy. You don't want to squander this surge, but rather, you need to understand that Mars is sacred; it is an important energy of change.

Self-knowledge leads you to exert yourself more authentically into the world. When you tap into that side of Mars, you find yourself empowered; knowing yourself more deeply, and capable of taking action more intelligently. When transiting Mars conjuncts your natal North Node, people enter who will inspire and see the strength within you, and help you bring forward your very best.

Harmonious transits of Mars to the Nodes bring energy, enthusiasm, and excitement. Childlike wonder and a spirit of play can help to align you with greater karmic blessings. The people you meet at this time have this same spirit of play, which makes them energizing company. Hard transits of Mars of the natal Nodes can bring a feeling of frustration. There may be a feeling of not being able to connect with the right people, who might help you move towards greater opportunities. Use this tremendous energy, and any frustrations you experience can be translated into effective action.

Jupiter in Aspect to the Nodes

Jupiter is the higher benefic, and the greatest of the ancient gods. And just like it sounds, Jupiter can represent big blessings. However, at times it isn't the 'blessings' part emphasized, as much as the more expansive side of this energy. More of what is too much already might be indulgent, but just enough used wisely, can be that much more bountiful.

Natal Jupiter in conjunction with the South Node signifies overindulgence and attracting "party people," especially when we are young. Consider the nature of the sign placement of Jupiter, to more fully explore the nature of the overindulgence. Consider going back to the section where we explored the sign placement of the South Node. Jupiter on the South Node will magnify that tendency many times over, the energy of the natal South Node that much more dominant within the chart.

Complicated relationships with teachers, mentors or professors in early life are possible. These types of people might leave one feeling wounded, or as if they were not treated fairly, for ultimately superficial reasons. There might also be notable experiences in childhood around discrimination rooted in race, ethnicity or religion. Perhaps it is you who looks back and realizes that you were taught xenophobic ideals, and might have behaved regrettably as a child because of it.

In *Further Along The Road Less Traveled* by M Scott Peck, Addiction is considered as a spiritual illness. According to Peck, we fall into addiction because our sensitive nature desires communion and connection with the Divine. The author draws the analogy that addiction is similar to the feelings of being in the womb, where you know you are connected to your environment, and feel a sense of protection.

Jupiter conjunct the South Node in the natal chart can represent a person, who would be sensitive in early life and might overindulge, either through substances or something else. They are people who want to be known as the life of the party. However, this identity is a mask, and they may not genuinely feel that these behaviors are making them happy. Ultimately, these behaviors invite us to consider our indulgence as a spiritual illness, as M Scott Peck called it, which desires communion and connection for genuine healing to occur.

Natal Jupiter conjunct the North Node is considered an especially fortunate placement, with a knack for attracting moral mentors and professors, especially in the higher learning environment. Opportunities at higher education might be available to you, that were not accessible to others in your environment. At times, this placement can suggest being an older student in said environment, thereby able to make the most of this time. This placement can also suggest career opportunities in academia, law, and politics being especially favorable, and occurring naturally.

An attraction to people of different cultures and languages might be present. It is these very people that can open up new worlds to you, in personal and professional ways. Matters of immigration and citizenship tend to run favorably, and you may likely learn another language as an adult. Opportunities to travel will likely continuously present themselves.

You may attract people who want to see you manifest the best in yourself, and have a more optimistic vision of you than you might realize for yourself. This energy will also help attract philosophical mentors, and those people who otherwise will cheer us up when we need. You grow in developing a more optimistic and enthusiastic approach to life. Jupiter has been considered the 'giver of gifts', so this is a placement of karmic blessings in this life.

Jupiter in harmonious aspect to the Nodes in the natal chart can suggest the optimism needed to try new things, meet new people, and forge genuine connections that open opportunities in life. This placement encourages us to prioritize happiness and use our innate talents, in the pursuit of our blessings. Hard aspects of Jupiter to the Nodes in the natal chart can suggest a more challenging time aligning with a higher, more loving vision for the life path. It may come about after a period of pursuing a different path all together, until trial and error, as well as overoptimism, help us to align with greater love and greater wisdom.

Transiting Jupiter in Aspect to the Nodes

With Jupiter, we begin to move towards the slower moving planets. Jupiter is one of the social planets. He normally takes about 12 years to travel all around the zodiac, spending about a year per sign in that time. The annual retrograde will happen at different intervals, but generally lasts about 4 months. Aspects of Jupiter are more rare than the other planets we have discussed so far. The sextile will happen twice in a 12 year cycle, along with the trine. The conjunction is just once every 12 years. The retrograde can increase the transiting aspect to up to 3 times, over the span of a few months. This gives us the opportunity to make the most of this expansive time.

A transiting Jupiter conjunction to one of the natal Nodes is an important astrological transit, considered an especially fortunate time. It only happens a few times in a lifetime.

When transiting Jupiter conjuncts the natal South Node, it is a major turning point in any life. It signifies a time of closing of karmic chapters and ending karmic ties. It brings a deep understanding what has served its karmic purpose in your life. It also tends to represent a major turning point for a lot of people; embracing a more practical understanding of Jupiter's energy.

Jupiter transiting the South Node is prone to manifesting its lower vibration. It denotes a time where we might be overdoing it, or going too far, in some area of life. The exact conjunction can represent a culmination moment. Jupiter conjunct the natal South Node can indicate the behaviors we are overdoing have reached their pinnacle, and come to an end. The pathway that we have been walking has reached its furthest point, and we now reach closure and move forward.

Jupiter also represents beliefs, so this placement can involve leaving behind a belief system that is no longer going to serve the future we are growing towards. In extreme cases, it can indicate leaving a religious tradition or community. A major shift of understanding, or an important ending can occur. Jupiter's reputation as the 'Great Benefic' suggests that the closures that do take place at this time are those which we almost immediately recognize as fortunate endings.

People may leave cities, homes, or even countries that they have lived in for years. Overindulgent behaviors might come to an end. There's an understanding, on a deep level, that something has served its purpose and for us, and it's okay to move on. In fact, we may see distinct advantages for allowing changes to happen now.

One of the more notable applications of this transit is how it allows deep forgiveness to occur. The kind that shifts our personal energy. It turns out to be a major turning point, signified by grateful feelings.

Transiting Jupiter conjunct the natal North Node is a standout time, that we might not fully appreciate in the moment. We aren't guaranteed to feel amazing. We need to see what's happening with the personal planets to consider what the overall mood might be. However, karmically speaking, it is a time when we connect with new people and welcome new opportunities. Consciously or not, we are being moved into alignment with a higher and more loving vision for our lives.

This transit can be subtle on the surface. It isn't always obvious which new people will be the ones that will open those big doors. Or, which casual connection will open a big opportunity. But in the fullness of time, when one looks back, they likely find that this was the 'seed moment'. It was during this conjunction that the stage was set for bigger, better, and more of what is good. It is an important time in life, when we meet people who will figure prominently in our success for a long time, even if not right away.

More personally, this is a time when we understand what direction we need to take to create greater blessings for ourselves. We may decide to pursue higher education. We may travel, and intentionally or not, it becomes an important pilgrimage. People who are foreign, different, or who represent different belief systems can hold special favor.

It could be a new religion or a new belief system; a new worldview could present itself to us at that time. Although Jupiter is not normally considered a romantic energy, it can bring romance as well. It is a time to welcome people, places, situations, and opportunities that create greater positivity, greater prosperity, and to move towards a life that's more inspired, more optimistic, and where all kinds of changes are possible.

This is a point in life where clarity comes in. It is a great time to start businesses and romantic relationships. Again, it might not be very obvious at the time, therefore, I encourage people to get out and about, to be active and meet people. Cast your net wide, and in unexpected ways, alignment with greater love and greater wisdom becomes accessible.

When Jupiter makes a harmonious trine or sextile to the Nodes, it is one's positive energy that brings practical advancement. The energy can take on greater subtlety, but there is an overall feeling that opportunities are available, and life is on your side. The hard T-square can represent moments of discomfort aligning us with a higher vision. It can also mean that, through realizing what doesn't feel right, we are move empowered to move towards what does.

Saturn in Aspect to the Nodes

Saturn is practical and realistic. Tangible and responsible. Saturn invites us to manifest, to honor the earthy incarnation by producing something we can be proud of. As much as its predecessor Jupiter can bring a bounty, Saturn will only give as much as you might give.

In aspect to the Nodes, Saturn can be a blessing, even when he feels like a burden, which he sometimes can. Saturn conjunct the South Node in the natal chart can be heavy and overbearing, giving a feeling of restriction in the early part of life. Especially complicated relationships with Elders, and sometimes the main paternal figure, like the father, might be there. This might also indicate feelings of serious obligations. Needing to grow up fast and take on responsibilities well above one's age can be a characteristic of this natal placement. To state the obvious; this isn't the easiest aspect to have in one's natal chart.

Saturn conjunct the South Node can indicate feelings in early life of being held back. Feelings of insecurity are sometimes understandable, given the responsibility. In rare instances, this can suggest immobility, sometimes brought on by fear of not being able to do it right. Limitations can also be felt in terms of one's truest expression. There might be a sense that one's own desires need to be restricted, in favor of what is required.

The larger lesson with Saturn is that faith is demonstrated through deeds. This lesson can be difficult for people with Saturn conjunct the South Node, because they might always feel like there's more to do, or that their best is not enough. The inner critic can inspire deep learning, and eventually inspire an appreciation of the higher, spiritual qualities of doing your best and surrendering the rest. The promise for those born with Saturn conjunct their South Node is that as they grow, they learn to focus their work ethic, and take practical steps to ensure happiness.

Saturn conjunct the North Node brings freedom through responsibility, not from responsibility. This is the placement of late bloomers, but they truly do grow to bloom bright. This placement attracts elders into our path, who are a part of helping us achieve something tangible in life. They help us learn the sacred lesson that 'anything worth having is worth working for'.

The natal placement of Saturn conjunct the North Node also denotes strong karmic alliances with bosses and people in positions of authority. They grant opportunities to work hard, and ultimately become an authority figure for one's self. In fact, this is a strong placement for someone that establishes a position of respect and recognition, slowly and surely, over the course of a lifetime.

They intuitively understand that it's not necessarily about where we are today, but about the small things we do today that are going to lead us into the future. One step at a time, they create a lasting legacy.

Transiting Saturn in Aspect to the Nodes

The more rare a transit is, the more defining it is. Saturn is a slow mover. He takes a full 28 and a half years to go all the way around the zodiac, spending approximately 2 and a half years per sign. The annual retrograde occurs for about 4-5 months. The conjunction occurs once every 28 and half years. If it happens during a retrograde, you'll get 3 passes over a 7-8 month period. The trine or sextile will happen twice over the almost 3 decade transit. The T-square is 2 times during that same period of time. If the retrograde is involved, these numbers can be tripled. Additionally, the Saturn station might be a factor in some occasions. This occurs when Saturn stays at a certain degree, within orb of the Nodes, over a period of weeks.

Transiting Saturn conjunct one of the natal Nodes is considered a notable and important life event. Its rarity itself will have it stand out. It always represents a big turning point, and important changes in life as well. Occurrences can be bluntly karmic; the job that ends, the new career opportunity, the personal realization. They all add up to manifesting, or tangible changes, in favor of something else.

Transiting Saturn conjunct the natal South Node always indicates a notable and defining ending. If we have been listening to life, and making changes along the way, they it need not be abrupt, until it is. This transit escorts us towards deeper maturity. In some way, we are taking ownership for what we have manifested in our lives, which is one of the defining traits of adulthood. We are being starkly honest with ourselves at this time, even if it is difficult or sometimes painful.

This is often a 'reality check' moment in our lives. A time when life asks us to take honest stalk of ourselves, and take responsibilities for what we have manifested. It can be a great moment, because it asks us to look at our lives and ourselves realistically, acknowledging where you are, and understanding where you may have been kidding yourself. In the best cases this presents a natural evolution, where we understand what needs to end, for a direction of greater maturity to be embraced. We might also be facing our own mortality. This is a reminder that this lifetime is finite, and that we should do what we can to take on our most fundamental responsibility; to own our happiness.

Saturn conjunct the South Node can signify a time of transition, but can also bring pain in endings. Saturn asks us to honor our incarnation. We are incarnated for a reason and there are specific lessons here in the 'Earth School' (as coined by Gary Zukuv) that, when embraced, will help us gain a sense of self-respect. If we aren't ready to embrace reality, this may be a difficult transition. It is the reality pill. The wake-up call leading to great changes.

I've seen people get clean and sober under this placement. I've also seen people change jobs, or leave friends and relationships behind. Where it is that we have been passing time, we realize how precious time itself is, and in taking action we honor this incarnation. This can also be a time when we realize what our responsibilities are, and admit if we have been living in a way that hasn't been honoring of our responsibilities.

For example, if we have become used to allowing another person to take care of us, or we entered into a relationship based on what the other person's financial situation was, this could be a time when that status changes. Consequently, something changes for us as well. We get honest about what really matters in notable ways.

Transiting Saturn conjunct the natal North Node is the opening of a doorway, from which new people carrying karmic blessings enter, and this involves moving us into a position of authority. This is when we are granted opportunities to become a boss in our own right. If we have been on a path that has been in alignment with a higher vision for our life, then this conjunction brings big opportunities, defined by more responsibilities and greater respect. This is the way the Universe directs us, so we can build a legacy that we can be proud of. Whatever it is that we do in any industry, this may be a time when we understand what we can do more of. This might not be easy, because there is work to be done, but there will be a 'flow', a rightness to what is changing now.

Though Saturn is not considered a romantic energy, it is an energy of commitment. This is also a time when we may attract people, who represent a more stable and secure future. Those who are looking for a stable, or perhaps traditional, partnership can find a mate with long term potential. Professional events provide the most promising pathways. Those in relationships might solidly the bond further.

The key to making the most of this transit is to cast your net as wide as possible. Saturn is an energy that is professional, but it doesn't necessarily mean it has to be stuffy or uptight. Engage life, be active, interact with others, and try new things. For example, if you're an astrologer, go to more astrology events. Whether personally or professionally, you'll likely make genuine connections with people, who figure prominently in you doing what it is that you've been called to do in this life.

When transiting Saturn conjuncts your natal North Node, pay close attention to your life, to see which way the winds are turning. Opportunities are going to show up, helping you see potential pathways towards stability and success. You are going to be lead towards building a future for yourself that feels stable and strong. A future that is likely to last a long time. A future that'll help you move up a ladder of success.

Harmonious aspects of transiting Saturn to the natal Nodes can indicate a time of easy acceptance of greater responsibility. It feels right, and that we are ready, for more authority. We may volunteer to take on more at this time, because we see the value in it and are up to the task. Hard aspects of the T-square might involve an extended amount of effort, without an immediate payoff. This can be frustrating, as we might feel that we are reaping less in life than our effort deserves. This transit shows us what we are willing to work for, and what is worth sacrificing for. If we make the most of this time, the harmonious aspect to the Nodes three years later may bring reward.

Uranus in Aspect to the Nodes

Uranus is the archetypal energy for shock and surprise. He prides himself on his revolutionary spirit and propensity towards revolt. So imagine coming into this life at a moment when this erratic and unpredictable energy is conjunct the South Node in the natal chart.

True rebellion is honoring the voice of your heart and living true to it. This is often the most revolutionary act for a soul to undertake, in a world filled with messages and conditioning about who we should be. However, natal Uranus conjunct the South Node can get caught up in false forms of expression, especially in the early part of life. The restless, edgy nature of this natal aspect can get caught up in displays of rebellion. Special care needs to be taken to cultivate consciousness in the early part of life, to prevent this energy from being regrettable, possibly experiencing the consequences for the turbulent actions of youth well into adulthood.

External and physical displays of ultra-uniqueness are possible with this placement, but it can take various extremes. Having a highly unusual way of dress or hair can easily be outgrown. Excessive body modification or tattoos may be more lasting. For those interested in permanent body art would be advised, if at all possible, to wait until at least the age of 30 before you start investing in major pieces on oneself, because the likelihood is you might change your mind.

Uranus conjunct the South Node can also indicate a sense of being difficult, or given to unreasonably rebellious behaviors. It's not that they are just for show. More likely, in the young life there was a strong sense of frustration, or feeling an intense lack of stability, that were seeking expression. There might have been feelings of being held back, possibly by circumstances that any sane person would want to to break free from.

With natal Uranus conjunct South Node, a person will come into this life with a strong desire to be an individual, and feel respected as an equal in the early environment. There are ways to be yourself and express yourself in a way that also honors the people around you. Finding balance between your inner drive for uniqueness, and the expectations of those around you, might be tricky. It will require patience, and a lot of experimentation, to learn how to express yourself authentically, giving the acceptance you seek from others.

The expression of uniqueness might not be simply superficial. Perhaps the way of seeing the world, and the ideas one holds, are considered unusual. It might feel as if you are misunderstood in your early life. Choosing contrary ideas for their own sake, and not out of a genuine dedication, is something to be cautious about. As one grows, there are like minded people to be found. Unique perspectives can be channeled towards making a meaningful contribution. However, constantly checking in with yourself, to be honest about your true motivations, is a healthy habit to cultivate.

When this energy is utilized well, the definition of freedom may evolve over the lifetime, so that what brings a sense of individuality changes dramatically from youth, in contrast to mid-life. These people are most likely to become unrecognizable, perhaps physically and personally. One caution though, if this dramatic shift occurs, is to ensure that this energy isn't then just projected outward towards attracting rebellious and unstable partners. If the work to incorporate a healthy sense of self-trust and self-acceptance is undertaken, outward displays of erratic behavior calms significantly.

Uranus conjunct the North Node in the natal chart invites one to truly becomes an authentic and brilliant person. It is a call to freedom, from the messages and conditioning of early life, and towards the peace of being an authentic version, aligned with a deep truth within. They will likely grow towards making a unique contribution in the world, or be seen as 'ahead of their time'.

166

These people must find the space and support to figure out who they are, if they are going to fulfill the intention of this lifetime.

Uranus conjunct the North Node may still indicate needless rebellion, but there is an understanding of this as experimentation. Supportive role models, who model independence, and emphasize the value of rational thought and social change, continuously show up throughout the lifetime to facilitate karmic blessings. People who are characterized as especially intelligent and free-thinking may be of special interest. Those whose existence in some way challenges the norms of society, whether in presentation or identity, are a source of special support and inspiration.

This is an energy of genius, and in ones own way, they are bringing forward a unique perspective to share. Utilizing new, independent technologies might be one way to engage with the masses. Important personal and professional connections might actually start online. A creative, scientific, and revolutionary mind evolves to the benefit of many, over the course of the lifetime. In fact, it is development within a niche that success, even fame, can be found.

The harmonious natal aspect of Uranus to the Nodes denotes someone who finds reward and opportunity the more willing they are to be unique. There tends to be encouragement towards a more rebellious ideal, especially in early life. There can also be rewards for intelligence, with opportunities to develop their ideas being available throughout the lifetime. These people may have opportunities to become 'visible' rather quickly, that they can parlay into lasting benefit. For example, the academic with that one breakthrough idea or the artist that is the one hit wonder, can be happy with the gains these successes continue to grant through the lifetime.

The hard T-square in the natal chart is an especially restless energy, that might find it challenging to understand its best expression. The ideas and inclinations can be so unique, that they are not understood by those around them. These people do find unique and niche communities of support as they grow, who join in and celebrate what others might call 'weird'. The right people will see genius and jump in on the rambling fun.

Transiting Uranus in Aspect to the Nodes.

Uranus is a slow moving planet, taking about 84 years to move all the way around the zodiac. About 7 years are spent in each sign over the course of the larger cycle. The retrograde of Uranus happens once a year and for about 5 months. The harmonious aspect will happen just twice each, for the sextile and trine, over the average course of the lifetime. The T-square will occur only twice. however, the retrograde ensures that each time represents an extended cycle, lasting up to 3 years, with up to 5 exact aspects during the extended transit. Given the rarity of Uranus transits to the natal Nodes, impressive life changes can happen at this time.

Uranus is unpredictable. Uranus shakes things up. He is a thunderstorm, washing and cleaning anything you don't need. It is dramatic, big and bold. Transiting Uranus in aspect to the Nodes can be a life-changer. The best advice during this transit is to practice trust, go with the flow, and allow whatever the Universe needs to move and to shake in life to find you.

Uranus conjunct the South Node involves sudden endings of situations that are no longer suited for your karmic path. People, places, things, environments, and dynamics that have served their purpose in your life will have to be let go of, in some cases instantly. Hanging onto things too tightly will make it that much more challenging to let go of.

However, the more one surrenders to this process of closure, the more refreshing it can be. This is an opportunity to start fresh, to begin again, and accelerate the karmic evolution towards greater love and greater wisdom. Focusing on where things are less than ideal would only get in the way. It is important to keep kindness at the forefront, where possible, but never at the expense of where freedom must now take place.

Uranus may unfold the identity, but at first, the characteristic is an emphasis on what is being left behind. The inherent nature of Uranus is truth. When transiting Uranus moves over the South Node, it is a dramatic truth that is revealed. The more we have been approaching our lives with awareness and a desire to cultivate consciousness, the less startling this truth will be. However, even for the best of us, the surprising nature of this aspect might feel excessive. Where we have been kidding ourselves, seeing only potential rather than stark truth, this could be a rude awakening.

The soul is asking for a rebirth within this lifetime. It is a new consciousness that is rushing in. Unpredictable external events occur if it serves the purpose of the soul's journey towards the fuller embodiment of greater love and greater wisdom. The more faith that can be practiced at this time, the quicker it is that new possibilities, perhaps never considered or unheard of before, start to pave the way.

Uranus will not shake free anything that doesn't need to be let go of, so when transiting Uranus conjuncts the natal North Node, bright, bold new beginnings show up for us. This remains as unpredictable as ever, but this transit can feel like big leaps forward, arriving out of nowhere. New people arrive, who carry a character of genius, brilliance, or perhaps the promise of the fresh start the soul is ready for. Big luck can take us by surprise. It is a special time.

Though Uranus is not considered a committed energy, the possibility of romantic experiences can surprise us at this time. They may be with people very different than what we have known before. Perhaps of a different religion, race, or gender than we previously allowed ourselves to consider before. They change us profoundly, from the inside out, leaving their mark on our soul.

A redefinition of self is happening at this time, as we become free of the expectations of others. Insights into whom the truest self is, understanding one's own genius, and clarity that allows you to follow your own unique path, regardless of what other people think about it, brings peace and courage. The larger, soul lesson is that being one's self is the surest path to greater peace, happiness, and fulfillment. The feeling of what you need to ensure you are living genuinely becomes abundantly clear, bringing with it the willingness to make changes to live that personal truth.

The harmonious transits of Uranus to the natal Nodes is a time when technology, or other experimental activities, can help one feel that their life is moving onwards and upwards. Whether for personal benefit or to change life's circumstances, it is by being willing to do things in an 'outside of the box' manner that surprising rewards can be found. An opportunity for visibility or notoriety can arise, in way that feels affirming and liberating. The hard T-square by transit can be a time of frustration and uncertainty. It is best used in the development of ideas, experimentation, and trying new things. Within the many things that don't work, sheer gold and big gains can be had. The other asset of this transit is that even when some experiments fall flat or seem like dramatic failures, they can be turned around towards remarkable success.

Neptune in Aspect to the Nodes

Neptune has been described as the higher octave of Venus. Like Venus, there is an association with art, music, and beauty. However, Neptune adds magic and mystery, accelerating the energy of beauty and making it a spiritual experience. Aspects of Neptune to the Nodes within a natal chart denote a major characteristic, which speaks to the soul path of an individual.

Natal Neptune conjunct the South Node can indicate over indulgence in escapist or dream like tendencies in the early life. This might sometimes be very literal; a need for extended sleep can be one propensity. Children with this placement would do well to have extra nap and sleep time, to fit this evolutionary need. These same escapist tendencies can also indicate a very strong imaginative faculty. Perhaps in childhood, wild tales were woven, that left people wondering how honest this child could be.

Perhaps, a need for medical treatment can lead to the inducing of unconsciousness, or treatments requiring anesthesia, are needed at key periods of time. Of course, most children with this placement will not manifest medical issues. However, given that Neptune is considered the patron of doctors, for its healing properties, they may find themselves engaging this industry in unexpected ways, perhaps through their own interest in the profession. In fact, past life memories as a doctor or healer may be present within.

There may be a sense that one is on a spiritual quest, or that there is great spiritual importance to their existence. In some cases, one might consider themselves to be a prophet, or have a special, spiritual message for the world. This might be an impetus that arises from within. It is also possible this is affirmed through the people surrounding the child in early life. The caution is that this energy must become embodied to count for something, or else the life can be spent in a cloud of denial. They can achieve the kind of spiritual reach they desire, once they make tangible plans and follow them up with action. And after that, balance it with humility, by recognizing that very energy of spiritual specialness is within us all.

This energy can also be highly sensitive and intuitive. So much so, that the early caregivers may find themselves in a period of uncertainty, as they seek to understand how to best address it. Sometimes the child needs to learn not to be overcome by their feelings. Developing skills to find healthy modes of moderation and balance can be useful.

Neptune conjunct the South Node might attract people in the early part of life who will encourage escapism, in less enlightened ways. It is also possible that there is a knack for attracting people who claim to be mediums or psychics. This may give way for a savior or guru; someone who can facilitate a mystical connection or magical communion. Over attachment to these types of people can happen, until the inner guru is found. As one enters adulthood, a rejection of these types of people might take place. Going to either extreme can occur, until one finds the savior within. It is also possible that early experiences with spiritual gurus are notable and disappointing, leading to the rejection of spirituality in later life.

Neptune conjunct the North Node in the natal chart invites a person to develop their spiritual and artistic skills over the course of a lifetime, finding role models along the way. These people may be given many opportunities to develop their artistic sensibilities, and can become accomplished in the fields of music, art, film, photography, and writing. Neptune speaks to illusion, and where it is that they find opportunities within these fields, they may find possibilities abound.

This is also considered a strong placement for compassion and altruism. We might find our ability to feel genuine empathy especially high now, which can lend itself to inspired actions. The giving quality of this placement can be self-sacrificing, but it is in a manner that ultimately feels that we are receiving in the process. Compassion can also lead us to think outside of ourselves, and in genuine giving, find greater karmic blessings in return. Opportunities within charities and non-profit organizations can bless the life in unexpected ways.

Regardless of what a person with this placement chooses to do, it would serve them well to incorporate the element of illusion as much as possible. Marketing materials can pay special attention to their artistic qualities in words and image. Excellent photographers, videos, and a presentation of their best self can enhance a sense of ease, as they seek to advance themselves professionally. Even the glamour of makeup or cosmetic surgery can provide avenues of success. They can make an impact on a wide scale, in front or behind the camera of their choosing. They themselves might become gurus and mystics in their own right, with insights and influence to reach masses. Where it is that they ground their ambition in spiritual purpose, they become that much more effective.

Those who have Neptune as signifier of karmic blessings in the natal chart, like a conjunction to the North Node would suggest, may have an ability to attract people who will encourage them to develop their artistic and spiritual sensibilities. Spiritual mentors, gurus, and healers hold special significance in the development of the soul path. An energy of miracles can sometimes surround these new people who enter, representing karmic blessings. It may feel as if people arrive out of the blue, and bring miracles to your life. Given Neptune is God of The Seas, it might feel as if these carriers of blessings have an elusive quality to them, able to arrive but also wash away. The impermanence of these bonds can be part of what can affirm a miraculous existence.

Natal Neptune in harmonious aspect to the Nodes can bring a special connection to music. These people may feel they have come into this life with heightened musical ability. Or perhaps there is music surrounding them in childhood. The poetic faculties can be high as well, lending to a predisposition towards imaginative writing. Opportunities to develop these tendencies are likely to present themselves, and with cultivation, can make for an adult recognized for their skill in these areas.

The hard T-square aspect invites one to remain diligent in their creative vision, even in the face of some external resistance or adversity. There is a delicate balance that needs to be reached, so that commitment remains, while a flexible approach is also entailed. The dreams or spiritual truth they have in early life might be different than the higher vision for their life. The discrepancy might require a period of acceptance. Bliss may be an aspiration, but it is ultimately a practical matter. For all that, these can be folks who are constant in their spiritual work, ensuring the tough questions that authentic spirituality asks for, find their answers.

Transiting Neptune in Aspect to the Nodes

Neptune takes 165 years to travel the zodiac, and will spend about 14 years per sign during that larger cycle. Transits of Neptune can last up to 3 years in total, as exact transits are repeated up to 5 times, due to his annual retrograde and overall slow pace. The harmonious trine and sextile combination will happen twice each over 165 years, which means that most people will experience just 1 combination over the course of a lifetime. The hard T-square is also likely a once in a lifetime event, though it happens twice over the 165 year cycle. Many people might never experience a conjunction of Neptune to one of the natal Nodes, so when it happens, it is considered a defining moment of the person's life.

When transiting Neptune comes along to conjunct the natal South Node, it is a time to face our own fantasies, and recognize where some have gone too far. There might be a period of indulgence in a heightened hope, followed by the stark realization that one has gone far enough with it. This can be a life defining wake up call, with the realization of what in our lives is an illusion, even that which might have felt was certain and secure.

In the most literal manifestation, Neptune represents water. This placement can bring problems with water, so special care should be taken in the home and outdoors. This might be a time when our internal water needs special care, so systems that flush out the organs, the lymphatic system, even our hormonal balance, may be something we need to take special care of.

In some instances, it may be people who leave our lives. Especially those who have played a healing role to us; doctors and other medical professionals, spiritual teachers and gurus, or perhaps someone characterized as artistic or poetic. With Neptune, those who are no longer part of the karmic evolution of the soul will wash away.

Before major life changes are made, people might sometimes need to reach rock bottom. With this transit, any escapist tendencies will be met head on. If we have gone too far with alcohol or other substances, this will be the turning point. Where it is that some other indulgence is now robbing us of genuine peace, we will face this as well. It need not be a life overhaul or a reckoning, though it might be.

Neptune has strong associations with faith, and the conjunction of transiting Neptune to the natal South Node can indicate that we admit to where we have accepted false gods into our lives. Whatever it is that we hold consistently in our minds, becomes a meditation. And whatever it is that we are meditating on, it is an act of worship.

The blessing of this transit is that it does ground our faith, but usually after facing the discomfort of self-knowledge. Where we have a discrepancy between the thoughts and objects we are worshiping though thought and energy, and what we believe a Higher Power to be, the contrast might be palatable and even difficult. In the best scenarios, this might be a time with some disappointment that quickly moves to acceptance. It can also be a time when we feel the hope we had had for others falls away, as we realize the difference between potential and reality is stark. It is from this space, that true acceptance can be found.

When transiting Neptune conjuncts the natal North Node, a near miraculous direction can open up. Our own spiritual prowess and psychic juice go on high. We might have an ability to attract new people at this time. They will be characterized as spiritual teachers, gurus, artists, actors, healers, mystics, and medics. Or perhaps one person will hold many of these roles. Their purpose in our lives is to awaken the abilities they bring, within our selves. Perhaps practical opportunities in these fields may present themselves. If you are already within these industries, this can be a time of heightened opportunity and success.

This might be a time when one's personal connection with a Higher Power feels like a driving force, opening up pathways and possibilities, in sometimes uncanny ways. An awakened artistic or mystical side can occur now. It can be that this interest is newfound; one suddenly realizes they want to learn an instrument or paint. For others, it can be a strong sense of connection to spirit provides guidance to the changes they desire to make.

One way of living can wash away at this time, in favor of something that feels more inspirational. Where it is that previous concessions were made, so that practical demands could be met, this will be when a more complete dedication to a pathway guided by spirit. Compassion can be especially heightened during this transit, and opportunities to find heart level connections can be well rewarded. Our meditative faculties and experiences strengthen during this transit.

The harmonious aspects of transiting Neptune to the natal Nodes bring a natural development and reward for artistic and spiritual abilities. We have the energy and motivation to create opportunities for ourselves, and thereby stay active to move towards what feels like a more inspired state of circumstances. For some, this might be spiritually meaningful, and that would be enough. For others, it is the more compassionate side of Neptune which arrises, encouraging us to make a positive difference in the lives of others, in the unique way we are called to.

The hard T-square of transiting Neptune to the natal Nodes can indicate a time of disillusionment or uncertainty. It can feel as if there is spiritual meaning we are yearning for, but not able to meet. The potential at this time is to continue to put in effort to move towards a more inspired future, which we are starting to glimpse. Squares always ask us for work, but the Neptune square can make the most effective actions uncertain. We may spend a lot of time and effort, only to find the fruits of our labors wash away. The potential of this energy is to have a deeper understanding as to how best be more effective, as we move closer to the dreams we have for our life. This aspect will lend itself to blessings, which arrive after this transit, and after the changes have been incorporated.

Pluto in Aspect to the Nodes

Pluto is the mythological God of The Underworld. Aspects of Pluto to the Nodes mean that, as part of the karmic pathway, a confrontation with that which others don't want to look at must take place. And just like the Underworld, the intensity of this natal aspect can make for someone with a notable and fated karmic road, filled with extreme highs and perhaps some lows, as well as a rebirth or 2 to boot.

Pluto conjunct the South Node in the natal chart can indicate an especially intense or complicated early environment. It might have felt like there were power games, manipulation, obsessions, or jealousy that marked the first part of life. There might have been a feeling of betrayal, or an awareness that things are usually more complicated than they seem on the surface. There might have been intense privacy, secrecy, and a feeling that there were things taking place that you didn't want others to know.

The South Node and its association with our most immediate past life that we are working through in this life, becomes a more pronounced mission, when Pluto is conjunct. There can be a feeling that many lives are being worked through in this life. Or perhaps that the most immediate past life was one where, there was a strong sense of unfairness for factors outside of one's control. In some extreme cases, there might be a desire for control now, to make up for the feelings of powerlessness that existed before.

The caution with this placement is that the first part of life might have a limited understanding of power, and what makes a person powerful. In an effort to feel a measure of control over their emotions or external circumstances, the person might pursue with obsession what they think might grant relief. This might involve seeking alliances, where they are able to be in charge. Or occupations that allow the indulgence of intense emotions and a feeling of power.

In some situations, there can be a sense of others draining you; of energy, of time, even money. Perhaps you find yourself drawn towards people who evoke strong feelings of betrayal or insecurity, which leave you feeling exhausted. The opportunity here is to bring a sincere and determined desire to become more conscious. It is in the diligent observation of one's self, and the tedious, diligent work of making more loving choices, that this energy becomes a source of great and undeniable power.

The opportunity with this placement is to come into this life with an intimate understanding of its complexities, and finding peace in the uncertainty. This is an energy of psychology, and where it is that you seek to cultivate a genuine understanding, the work will be rewarded. Past life memories in key professions might draw you now. Therapy, to those who have experienced profound trauma. Surgery, which requires complicated, yet detached knowledge of our physical processes. Even dealing with those, who have otherwise been rejected by society. These are all areas where there is the potential to bring an intuitive understanding and focused commitment to facilitate meaningful change.

Pluto is the mythic Phoenix, rising from the ashes. Pluto conjunct the South Node in the natal chart is someone who has come into this life, within circumstances that are to be transcended. The impetus is to rise, but in order to do that, you have to first admit that there are ashes in which you stand. It is then that the work can be done to become a Phoenix in your own right. In this way, their wings, and every brilliant color within it, is well earned.

Natal Pluto conjunct the North Node is, in contrast, the Phoenix fully owning its wings and learning to soar. This is someone who has come into this life with determination and focus. Allowing full flight over the coarse of this lifetime. They might sometimes take for granted the magnetism and presence that they hold. Regardless of the appearance, and whether or not it conforms to their societies standard of beauty, there is something hypnotic about them. They are leaving behind the perfunctory, and embracing the real.

Those with natal Pluto conjunct the North Node are able to attract people, who have a deeply transformative effect on one's life. Bonds with others will be anything but superficial. There is the ability to see to the core of people, and find meaningful connections, from the inside and out.

Anytime you care about someone, you are changed by them, and facilitate change within them. These are people within whom powerful karmic bonds are shared. They also facilitate karmic blessings. It is the emotional intimacy and honesty you cultivate with others, which allows for an almost therapeutic effect, where the 2 take turns providing insight into the other. These may be platonic relationships, but certainly romantic relationships as well. People who have Pluto conjunct the North Node can attract romantic partners, who are like therapists. Therapy and psychoanalysis is covered by Pluto.

Pluto is also God of Wealth, and as part of stepping into your power, you uncover a sense of wealth. Wealth will likely be defined in deeply personal terms. This natal aspect indicates the ability to build great wealth over the course of their lifetime. It isn't really about the money. Rather, it's about being true to you, which in turn leads to great prosperity.

Harmonious aspects between Pluto and the Nodes in the natal chart brings opportunities to develop focus and determination, to fulfill a meaningful destiny. Magnetism is something that needs time to develop, but once the skill is learned, makes a meaningful difference to the life path.

The hard T-square aspects can denote constant motivation, but also insecurity, towards aligning with a higher vision for one's life. There might be a constant sense of inner frustration. The determination to align with a higher vision and one's own will might seem to contrast at times. There is likely going to be a moment in life when one path is transformed, in favor of a completely different life path. It is when the will is surrendered, and trust in the Universe is cultivated, that greater power is found.

Transiting Pluto in Aspect to the Nodes

Pluto takes about 248 years to circle the Sun, and during that time will spend about 21 years per sign, though because of his oval pathway, he will spend more years in some signs than others. This slow pace of Pluto indicates that his transits are rare. Most of us may never experience some of these transits. The harmonious aspect might be just once in a lifetime, with this transit occurring about every 40 years. The T-Square hard aspect occurs every 124 years. During a transit, and the extended, annual retrogrades Pluto comes with, there can be up to 5-6 exact moments over the course of up to 4 years.

Pluto transits to the natal South Node or natal North Node are always a time of profound changes. The planet of rebirth will facilitate renewal, one way or another. The nature of the aspect tells us how it might be experienced. Regardless of whether we interpret events as good or bad, they are fated, and always necessary. Considering that this cosmic event occurs so rarely, there are many who might never experience a conjunction of Pluto to one of their natal Nodes.

When transiting Pluto conjuncts the natal South Nodes, we will have no doubt what has served its purpose. The underlying truth to any hope or illusion will be revealed. We are asked to release the superficial. What's left is honest and more valuable to us than we could fully appreciate, especially in the middle of the transit. While the transit can be challenging, the outcomes can bring tremendous self-knowledge and fated change. On the other side of this transit, we experience gratitude to have something lasting and real in our lives.

One of the most notable aspect of transiting Pluto conjunct the natal South Node has to do with endings. People, places, things, situations, and relationships can end. In some cases, there is pain associated with some of those endings. Perhaps feelings of betrayal, manipulation, or unfairness might characterize this time. However, on the other side, and perhaps in the midst of this time, there is a sense that what is ending has served its karmic purpose in the life path. On the other side of this transit, we start moving towards more genuine alliances with others.

There may be a sense of burning bridges behind you. A major shift, characterized by what is ending, is taking place. We can make this transit infinitely more difficult when we try and hold on too tightly. The most effective approach is surrender. It is at this time that the Universe is attempting to move us forward. Anything that weighs us down or gets in the way of our soul's evolution, must leave at this time.

Although some of these closures might be painful at the time, they might not exclusively be so. Many times, the closures now bring a sense of peace. There might have been a slow burn towards this change. When it comes, it brings relief.

Any new people that enter at this time may come with complicated circumstances. The people you attract now will likely evoke powerful feelings within you, designed to help you release patterns or long held trauma. They may evoke your early life or childhood, and through the intensity of the experience, you are encouraged to get to the root of the pain, so that you can release it for good. In this way, the shifts now will put you on a new path towards healthier relationships. But first, you may have to recognize what is keeping you from the type of evolved love you deserve.

Pluto also connects with wealth and finances, so this aspect can indicate a change in financial conditions. Pluto is about letting go of the superfluous, so financial change doesn't necessarily mean that our prosperity will change, or that we will lose money and become poor. However, it can mean that a stream of income may come to an end. However, Pluto conjunct the South Node can bring an ending to a financial matter, perhaps a challenging one related to a settlement we had been hoping for, or a loan we have been paying off. This aspect can bring fruition, and thereby closure.

Being a reborn Phoenix, ascending from the ashes, is what Pluto signifies. Ultimately, we are rising above, more amazing and stronger. However, we have to trust the process. Releasing over attachment to material things, people, or any circumstance that's been cosmetic, is the best way to ensure we can ascend forward from here.

Transiting Pluto conjunct the North Node represents a time of profound metamorphosis. We will attract people into our lives, who will have a deeply transformative effect on us. They serve as a catalyst towards more sweeping changes. Some of these experiences might be intense, but we embrace them for our own evolution. Regardless of whether these connections last, they leave an indelible mark. They make us better.

Some of these experiences will be characterized by profound intimacy. There might be a physical side of it. Emotional vulnerability is what ultimately allows the energetic changes to occur. Physical changes are possible now, with a stronger version of yourself emerging. You are connecting to a core of power within, and your appearance might change in tandem with the inner change.

We might be inspired to undergo therapy at this time, perhaps for the first time. Psychoanalytic processes can be very beneficial now, as we might attract someone who can help make sense of the changes taking place, and make the most of them. You may attract bankers, surgeons, or detectives, as part of understanding your truth and embracing the profound changes on offer now.

It is going to be up to us to embrace that pathway forward, leading us to understand who we are more deeply. The only thing that makes Pluto painful is attachment, so if you don't attach yourself too firmly to any situation or any material things, then Pluto can bring forward its absolute best for you: being reborn as a truer version of yourself. As a more authentic and stronger version than you knew before.

The harmonious transit of Pluto to the natal Nodes is an empowered time. We are granted opportunities to transform our lives, and based on our own effort, move towards an understanding of what it means to be authentically ourselves. We get more honest with ourselves about what we would rather be doing, and find opportunities to hone in on a more favorable direction.

The T-square hard aspect can be a time of hard lessons that change us deeply. We can attract particularly complicated alliances, which might frustrate us. However, in doing the work that change requires, we are made a greater force in the world. It is the hard aspect that propels change, through our own determination for changed circumstances. This transit brings hard lessons that we come to see as a 'blessing in disguise'.

Quick Reference Guide

North Node Through The Signs

Aries- Life will constantly ask you to trust yourself, trust your passion more than anything, trust your inspiration and trust what it is that is fun for you. An entrepreneurial spirit can open karmic blessings.

Taurus- Life will lead you towards a more grounded and diligent approach in your goals. It is in developing the 5 senses and a greater sense of being 'present', whether through formal meditation or philosophy, that larger blessings open up.

Gemini- Developing spontaneity, finding your voice, and expression in the moment, about being spontaneous in your expression. New experiences and ideas can allow your creativity to spark. Karmic gifts open when communication is developed.

Cancer- Learning to through emotions and feelings, separating fear from intuition. There's a very powerful sensitivity and life is going to put you in situations where you have to develop your intuition and understand how fear is guiding some of your instincts.

Leo- Acknowledgment that there is something within you that is worthy of shining and being seen. The sign of Leo rules the heart and it has to do with what lights up your heart as well. Karmic gifts open when genuine confidence grows.

Virgo- Being analytical in your approach and doing your background work is covered here. It is through diligence and practice that expertise is developed, which then opens greater blessings.

Libra- Partnerships of all kinds are especially beneficial, allowing you to open up greater opportunities and happiness in your life. Genuine sharing and consideration of other perspectives broadens your horizons.

Scorpio- Issues of trust and intimacy bring the greatest learning opportunities. Learning to see behind the superficial and instead see what is truly essential to your life allows for greater authenticity. You will likely experience at least one major rebirth in this lifetime.

Sagittarius- Asks you to have something that you are enthusiastic about. Life is going to ask you to take on an adventure, which opens larger blessings. New ideas and people from foreign lands open up karmic blessings and new opportunities.

Capricorn- A very special sense of self-respect that comes from having a vision or a goal and sticking to the process long enough to see it through. Honoring the process of manifestation and you reap the rewards.

Aquarius- Understanding your uniqueness in relation to others. Contributing to a joint endeavor our cause. Humanitarian and social awareness can create bigger opportunities for blessings and happiness in your own life. These people can have a large social impact.

Pisces- Connecting to your own intuition. Developing your psychic and artistic energies. It is by cultivating your own connection to source energy, and bringing that forward through some spiritual or artistic manifestation, that larger blessings open.

North Node Through The Houses

1st House- A strong sense of self, of mission, and self-expression will guide the life. The soul often has a sense of destiny, and a soul level awareness of what it is here to do. In honoring what matters to you most and first, you open larger blessings in your life.

2nd House- Life will provide many opportunities to provide for yourself, work on your own behalf, and know your power to create prosperity. It is in consciously cultivating possessions and deciding what is worth the money and what isn't, that larger blessings open.

192

3rd House- Opportunities and blessings come when you develop your voice, develop your perception and develop your mind. You will be asked to find out what is your voice in this lifetime, how is it that you will share it and how is it that you are going to express yourself.

4th House- Understanding your family, your roots, your culture and identity, and what that's going to mean for you on a fundamental level, a level of your physical ancestry. A strong sense karmic blessings, perhaps delivered through family connections.

5th House- Trusting your passion, acknowledging or figuring out just what your passion is, and then going with it and developing it. Taking risks and trusting your instincts bring karmic rewards. Children in your life can provide special blessings, and open up larger opportunities.

6th House- It is in focusing on the smaller moments of your day that bigger blessings follow. There tends to be fortunate connections made with co-workers, doctors, even hairdressers. There are plenty of opportunities to develop skills and acquire more work. Larger blessings come when you develop expertise in one area.

7th House- There are many opportunities to develop contacts, share ideas, and contemplate the interactions in your life. As the house of partnerships, it is in aligning with others that karmic rewards open. These people will often develop strong bonds that bless them personally and professionally.

8th House- Shared resources and financial institutions. This is a strong placement for developing wealth, practical and emotional. There is a sense of being truly cared for by others, and cultivating a deep perceptive into self and others. The law of attraction, occult practice, and self-exploration bring rewards.

9th House- The soul evolves most when it is allowed to consider new new ideas, new people, new languages as well new cultures. Practical opportunities to travel, pursue higher education, as well as favor in legal matters. Professors and mentors of all kinds bring karmic blessings.

10th House- We are asked to consider success and become more visible in the process. Bosses and authority figures can be especially helpful. There will always be more opportunities to move towards your larger goals. It is in becoming an authority in your own right that larger rewards open.

11th House- Broader identity, organizations, unions, or fellowships that you might belong to hold strong karmic connections. Using your alliances towards larger, shared aims makes for the most success. You might be presented with opportunities in mass media or to make a social impact.

12th House- Life is asking you to look at what is really happening behind closed doors. There may be time spent alone or in isolation, sometimes through your own choosing. Meditation and with connecting to source are ways in which you open up karmic blessings. This is a lifetime to reap rewards that might have been delayed in a previous lifetime.

South Node Through The Signs

Aries- Being mindful about seeking the adrenaline rush and outward shows of courage. The true act of courage is living in a way that grants inner trust. Being overly impressed by shows of physical strength can elude the work of inner strength in early life. Moving away from solely relying on yourself and knowing you are not alone in the world.

Taurus- Missing the spiritual dimension to life, and thinking that only your 5 senses are what is 'real'. Being mindful not to judge yourself or others based solely on outward shows of prosperity. Stubbornness can be barrier towards cultivating larger blessings, until you learn to evolve and grow.

Gemini- Being mindful of the power of communication. There might have been moments in the early life, or a past life, where gossip and 'talking too much' lead to hurt feelings in yourself and others. Complicated relationships with siblings might show in early life. Speaking with greater integrity moves the energy in the direction of blessings.

Cancer- Moving away from sentimentality and from a false sense of security that familiarly for its own sake might bring. Moving out from 'home' and into the world to be seen in the broadest sense. This placement can indicated a complicated relationship with your parents, the mother in particular, where karmic bonds are especially strong.

Leo- An unhealthy ego might express itself in early life. We all need a healthy ego to remind us we are worthy, but it's when we rely too much on the opinions of others that we move in a precarious direction. There may be a sense of 'deserving' the best before you have earned those rewards.

Virgo- Moving away at being overly preoccupied with small details, as to miss the larger, more inspired vision. There can be the tendency to be overly analytical, worrisome, or to create stress through one's own thoughts. The stomach might be especially sensitive in early life, where food allergies can resolve themselves as you grow older.

Libra- Co-dependant relationships, or defining oneself simply by whom you are associated with. The early life could have brought unhealthy examples of partnerships and love in general, but the opportunity is to develop a strong enough sense of self and allow that to fuel future, more enlighten bonds.

Scorpio- There may be an acute sense of the extreme experiences of life, including the real pain and complex emotions people can feel. Early life experiences where power struggles might have factored in, whether financial or emotional, can encourage self-reliance and more grounded relationships.

Sagittarius- Moving away from being righteous and about being overly ideological. It is about moving away from just looking at the world from a very rigid perspective, a very limited philosophical perspective, and it is about moving away from understanding the world simply by what you've been told it to be.

Capricorn- An overt sense of success as performance. Authority figures might have featured in early life, including complicated relationships, perhaps with the main paternal figure. Moving away from a desire for reward and accolades for its own sake, and towards a life that find joy in familiar, more personal moments.

Aquarius - Early life can include eccentric or rebellious behaviors for show, because there is inner fear of honoring the intuition. You may get trapped in displays of individuality for its own sake. Stubborn attitudes and rigid philosophies can be transformed towards more heart-centred living.

Pisces- Pursuing feelings of bliss as escapism. In its lowest manifestation, addictions of different kinds can become evident. The soul desire is to ultimately live a life that is more grounded in action, not simply intention. Some musical ability, or strong intuitive abilities, can show themselves in childhood.

South Node Through The Houses

1st House- An over emphasize on self, without consideration of other perspectives, might be a tendency that shows in early life. There might have been a need to be self-reliant much early than is normally expected. The soul is moving towards appreciating the wide differences of opinions and being better for exchanging ideas.

2nd House- Being overly occupied with possessions and outward displays of luxury or wealth. This might indicate hoarding tendencies in early life, as there might be past life memories of financial loss. The opportunity here is to remember how much of the world is illusionary, and finding stability in change.

3rd House- Complicated relationships with Siblings and Cousins in early life. Strong karmic bonds with neighbours and early teachers might exist. There may be a tendency towards over-curiosity, or a lack of ability to focus on. A single task. There is the tendency to be a "Jack of all trades, master of none".

4th House- An over-reliance on all things familiar, and a fear of new experiences can sometimes show itself in early life. There is a desire to acquire "creature comforts", and perhaps overindulgence in "comfort foods". The tendency towards isolation is here as well, until the energy is raised towards outward experiences.

5th House- A focus on child-like fun might over extend itself long after childhood is over. There can be a performance element, that needs to learn to arise form a more genuine place. Gambling and other risks not well thought out may be a characteristic that shows in early life, before perspective is cultivated.

6th House- An over reliance on small rituals may show in early life. There can also be a near obsessive tendency to control small details. A need to work at a younger age than usual, and a complicated dynamic with co-workers can show itself before greater depth is cultivated.

7th House- Strong Karmic bonds with partners, a sense of replaying past patterns within your one on one personal and professional alliances. This placement can either indicate marriage taking place very early, or much later in life. Energetic responses to potential partners can be instant.

8th House- Moving away from sharing, being dependent or relying on other people or institutions for survival. There can be particularly complicated or painful early experiences of power dynamics. There may be a sense of not wanting others to have power 'over' you, which can fuel a desire for healthy independence.

9th House- Early life travels that led to defining, karmic experiences. There may sometimes be early interactions with legal matters that make a strong impression. There may be a resistance to higher education. Strong karmic ties with professors and those in legal professions may show in early life.

10th House- There is a movement away from achievement, or having public status for its own sake. There may be early example of people who misused authority. There may be fame or notoriety in early life, or examples of the downside of public visibility. An over reliance on the acknowledgment of others will be replaced with inner acceptance later in life.

11th House- Over identifying with a group and committing your identity in accordance to who you know. Allowing others to define you. Participating in group endeavor for personal gain. Early experiences with peers might be the proverbial "bad influence". Complicated bonds with friends can appearing early life, until self-reliance is cultivated.

12th House- There might have been a circumstances that led to isolation for periods of time in early life. Sometimes this is as a result of parental involvement in intensive spiritual practices, and other times it may be due to a medical condition. In some instances, early life can feature examples of people who created pain through living in addiction.

Acknowledgements

Thank You to my Fabulous Friends, Fans, Superstars, Clients, and Students. Your trust means so much to me. Sharing this journey with you makes it that much more rewarding.

Thank you to my family, spiritual and physical. My amazing parents Shahnaz and Saif, my brother Fareed and Sister-In-Law Jenn, and all their animals, who are my nieces and nephews. My many extended family members, especially my aunt Shireen, whose wisdom shows up in my work almost every day. To Manuel and Biggie, my little family that means so much to me. Thank You all for your unconditional love, always.

Nikki Gonzales is the artist who designed the cover of this book. I am forever grateful she shares her creativity with me and with the world.

Thanks to my astrologer friend Andy for his inspiration, encouragement, support and editorial help, even when he and his Galactic Centerish Sagittarius Mars are ranting that they don't agree with anybody's ideas (including mine!). Andy is one of my very best astrology friends. We are often seen hanging out at astrology conferences together. I consider myself very fortunate to have an amazing person like Andy as a friend.

To the astrologers I meet at conferences or online, and to the many astrologers, who practice quietly at kitchen tables around the world. We are all part of one community. We are all family, and to you I send my most heartfelt gratitude and encouragement. It is a path of absolute dedication to a voice of inner authority within that leads us to this practice. As much as you give, as much as the rewards are there.

Credits & Further Readings

He So Knoweth Thyself, Ibn'Arabi

The 3 Books of Occult Philosophy, Cornelius Agrippa

Noah Frere, RPT, Astronomologer (Instagram @astronomologer; https://www.etwellnessdirectory.com), Astrophysics Masters candidate at University of Tennessee, Knoxville

Further Along The Road Less Travelled, by M. Scott Peck

The Seat of The Soul, by Gary Zukuv

French Vanity Fair named Nadiya Shah one of the top 12 astrologers on the planet, crowning her a pioneer in video astrology. She is an Internationally Syndicated Astrologer, Author, Media Personality, and is one of the few people in the world to hold an M.A. in the Cultural Study of Cosmology and Divination, from the University of Kent, United Kingdom.

Nadiya's Book, *The Body and The Cosmos* and *Prayers To The Sky* both debuted as a #1 New Release in New Age Astrology on Amazon. Her school *Synchronicity University* teaches astrology online and worldwide. Nadiya's wildly popular Youtube channel, *nadiyashahdotcom*, is one of the most watched Astrology channels in the world.

Visit Nadiya's website at:

NadiyaShah.com

Printed in Great Britain
by Amazon

11750464R00119

The Universe is Wise and Loving

The Nodes of The Moon In Astrology

By Nadiya Shah